The Essence of the Korean Buddhist Practices

6 Ways to the Heart

The Essence of the Korean Buddhist Practices

6 Ways to the Heart

Association of Korean Buddhist Orders

introduction

A Way Home

Life is like a journey. We pack our bags in excitement and anticipation, and gingerly face the unknown wonders gently unfolding in front of us. The journey is joyously rewarding as new people, new things and new happenings fill our senses with an unfamiliar beauty. However, mysteriously, the beauty of these new wonders fades rapidly, no longer offering the thrills and delights they used to. As the journey progresses, the sense of adventure is replaced by the overwhelming feeling of world-weariness. Our minds become burdened with the fear and worries associated with our decisions, for now we know that dangers lurk at the corner of each new road. Streaked with the dirt from the road, speckled with insect bites and sore with hunger, cold and tiredness, we suddenly stop and ask ourselves, “What am I doing here? It is time to go home.”

Ah, home sweet home—fragrant flowers and chirpy bird songs, jolly faces with no trace of malice, a safe harbor from the stormy wind and rain. A belly full of warm, delicious food and a cozy bed—the thought alone would put a smile on our face.

However, the way home is not as straightforward and trouble-free as we would like. The journey home is filled with detours that are tricky to negotiate. When we turn home-ward, we suddenly find ourselves as far away from home as deeply as we miss it. Some might even ask themselves, "Where is my home?"

If you are lost on your way home, I would like to recommend looking for a reliable guide instead of blindly bumbling along the way. If you meet a guide who knows the way well, who knows how to navigate the sometimes treacherous curves and how to avert disasters on the way, you will get to the home of your dreams much faster and easier than you expected. Here in Korea, there are people who are happy to walk the path home with you. They are the descendents of the original guide, Sakyamuni Buddha. If you can trust the warmth in their smile and the sincerity in their eyes, I would like to encourage you to hold the hands that are eagerly extended to you.

The steps you take with the guide will make your heart flutter because it is the path you are always meant to take. You may need to pluck up the courage that exists deep inside you to take that first step. Because the path is new to you, as it always was, and as it always will be.

Springtime in my hometown,
Deep in the mountain flowering with
Blossoms of peach and apricot,
Tender buds of azalea.
Yearning for the days of innocent play
Frolicking in the lush feast of vibrant hues,
Alongside birds and flowers,
Weeping willows gently swaying
Along the gurgling brook,
In the southerly wind from the green field.
Yearning for the days of innocent life
In my hometown.

Lyric by Lee Won-su
song composed by Hong Nan-pa

Contents

What is Buddhist practice?

How is your mind?

Buddhism is the teachings of the Buddha. What are the teachings of the Buddha? It would be difficult to illuminate the whole body of his richly diverse lessons on the limited pages in this short booklet. However, it can be safely surmised as the teachings on suffering; the causes of suffering; the cessation of suffering, and; the path to the cessation of suffering. This is also called the Four Noble Truths.

The Buddha's teaching starts with the universal, all pervasive truth of suffering, which can be divided into mental and physical suffering. Physical suffering usually consists of the unpleasant sensations and pain from disease, cold, hunger and thirst; mental suffering is the emotional and psychological anguish of depression, sorrow, fear and anxiety. It is the emotional and psychological distress which the Buddha has exhaustively explored and provided painstakingly meticulous answers to. The Buddha preached in the *Anguttaranikaya*:

"Bhikkhus, there are two diseases. What are these two? They are the disease of the body and the disease of the mind.

Bhikkhus, there are many people who enjoy 1 or 2 years without suffering from physical illness. There are people whose bodies remain healthy for 3, 4, 5, 10, 20, 30, 40, or 50 consecutive years. There are even people who have never been beset by illness until they die. But, Bhikkhus, it is truly rare to meet somebody whose mind has never been ailed by the sickness of mind, not even for a short while."

Are you grieving the loss of a beloved?

Are you angry with someone who hurt you?

Are you burning with the desire for what you want but cannot have?

Are you afraid of the future that may hold what you fear?

Are you depressed and blaming yourself for failing to achieve your goal?

Are you unable to make any decision, hopelessly tangled in the web of complicated thoughts?

Are you living your life as if being helplessly tossed around like a raft lost at sea?

Are you feeling burdened by life itself?

If the answer is yes to any of these questions, your mind is agitated and you need the medicine of the Buddha's teachings. Just like the wounds of the body, the wounds of mind deepen and fester if left unhealed. However, if self-healing does not come easily, seek out the descendents of the Buddha. They know precisely what causes such distress; moreover, they are well versed with the remedies for suffering and have ample experience skillfully administering them.

Poisoning and antidotes

If you are discontent with your life right now, you need to understand why and how your life has come to that by carefully and patiently disentangling the multi-layered phenomena that are your life. The Buddha says, "Everything arises and is maintained by conditions. All conditioned phenomena cease to exist once the sustaining conditions perish."

There are no consequences without causes. If we are suffering from unsatisfying and unpleasant situations, we have planted seeds in the past that have caused those unwanted situations to arise in the present. If these undesirable situations continue to besiege us, that means we are continuing to fuel the fire under the mental cauldron of our mind.

If we ingest rotten or toxic food, we suffer from abdominal pain. The pain would subside as the body purges the bad food by vomiting or by taking medicine. However, it would not work unless we stop eating spoiled food. The process of curing the mind of suffering is similar. The Buddha taught that the suffering of mind is caused by the three toxins of greed, anger and ignorance. Poisoning by any of these three toxins sets off torturous miseries in the mind and its contamination spreads to other people around us as well.

If the mind is in pain, it is caused by the arising of greed, anger and ignorance in the past. If the suffering still consumes us, that means our mind is still being disturbed by the jittery agitations of greed, anger and ignorance. Without being free from the three poisons, we can never be liberated from suffering.

The most vigorously dominant poison of all three is greed. What is greed in Buddhism then? Buddhism defines the six faculties of sensory perception as eye, ear, nose, tongue, skin and brain, each of which performs the functions of seeing, hearing, smelling, tasting, feeling and thinking. This process of sensory perception leads to the feelings of like and dislike. The perceived experiences are then stored in the consciousness, which result in the desire to repcat the experiences that are registered as pleasurable.

For example, you happen to walk through a forest and your eyes rest on a beautiful flower. You stand there for awhile captivated by its brilliant red color and lovely fragrance. Years roll by and you pass through the same wood again. Your eyes will be unconsciously sweeping the forest in search of the sight of that charming flower from years ago. This longing to experience the sensations of pleasure in color, shape, sound, scent, taste, touch and thought; the desire to perpetuate the pleasure if you are already experiencing it, and; the desperate quest to own it so as to ensure the continuation of pleasure in the future—it is what is called greed in the Buddhist context.

The object of greed is compounded from the elemental components of sight, sound, smell, taste, touch and thought, which interweave in manifold combination and construct diverse concepts such as love, prosperity, honor, power or existence. It was 'a brilliant red color' and 'a lovely fragrance' that originally captured the eyes and the nose, but later, it becomes 'the flower' that we continually seek to re-experience.

We feel exuberant when we obtain the object of our desire, labeling it as 'ours.' If the object of our greed is taken away from us, we feel despondent. If the desired object is difficult to own, or the attempt to own it is thwarted by somebody else, we get mad. The sadness and anger are diseases of the mind. Some may say, "I feel elated when I accomplish something I like. If I keep making efforts and keep winning, can my life be one big never-ending succession of gratification?"

The Buddha's answer to this is "no." Does anyone ever achieve the capability to gain everything he or she wants? More often than not, things simply fall short of our expectations. Even if one manages to possess the superpower of getting everything he or she wants, the joy does not last. There is no guarantee that what becomes 'mine' will stay that way. More importantly, what we covet is in the state of permanent flux. All the flowers in this world eventually and inexorably wither. We forget this, and the greed and desire control us and we are perpetually at the mercy of tumultuous feelings of regret and frustration.

Then, where does this grasping come from? The Buddha said that such fervent craving, which 'enslaves us as compellingly as desperate thirst for water', stems from ignorance. We forget that 'everything in this world constantly changes' and lose sight of the truth that there is no

fixed entity of 'I' and that nothing permanently stays as 'mine.' This is ignorance, the state of the mind in dull stupor. We fail to grasp the reality as it truly is because we ignore the fact that everything is in a constant state of flux. We erroneously construct 'I' as a subject and 'others' as objects. We are helplessly caught in the conflicts between these two misconceived axis, generating delight, longing, hatred, depression, heartache, panic and despair in the process. We often just accept this dichotomy as our life.

The Buddha gave extensive instructions in order to cure people of the three poisons. Buddhist practice is the process of following the Buddha's words to be free from pain, anxiety and discontent by removing the three poisons of greed, anger and ignorance and restoring the happiness and joy innate to all sentient beings.

Emulating the Buddha

In Korea, Buddhists put their palms together in greeting or parting and wish each other, "May you become the Buddha."

The Buddha was the happiest being in the world because he was enlightened to the true reality of existence in its entirety, completely free from all compulsions and delusions. He was no longer fuelled by desire, nor did he tremble with fear, neither was he choked with misery and he was never burdened with sleepless nights. Having transcended all agonies and aches, the Buddha was a serene, gentle, pure and generous being. He did not lament the by-gone past, nor was he troubled by the future yet to come. He cherished the present and delighted in the life existing in each and every moment, like a string of pearls to be savored and grateful for. Buddhists in Korea are praying for each other, that their lives be full of peace and happiness attained by the Buddha.

But, we cannot become a Buddha by the wish alone. A mindful of miseries and agonies do not transform themselves into wisdom and compassion without a change of action. If we wish to live as happily and contentedly as the Buddha himself, we need to learn how to turn our actions into the Buddha's own by applying moral conduct (sila), meditative concentration (samatha) and wisdom (vipassana) to our everyday lives.

Human actions can be largely divided into three categories: actions committed by body, speech and mind. All actions give rise to consequences. Good actions result in desirable outcome, bad actions lead to evil conclusions. If our bodies are inflicting violence on others, stealing other people's properties, or if our bodies are overwhelmed by lust and engaged in sexual misconduct, be assured that the consequences will return to us. If our mouths are lying, spreading fabricated stories, slandering others behind their backs or spewing obscenities, afflictions are not far away from us. If our minds are restless with unfulfilled craving, overcome with hatred or so engulfed in its own thought that it fails to see plain facts, make no mistake that we are soon to be haunted by distress. If we wish to protect ourselves from unbearable pain and suffering, we must discontinue right here and right now, and get into the habit of refraining from such activities. Act with discipline and moderation, speak gently and honestly and think calmly and carefully. In Buddhism, applying such principles to all our actions is called the practice of the precepts or sila.

However, detaching ourselves from wrongful actions is not enough. Our mind is easily overpowered by greed and anger, easily turning us into a devil in a flash. Why does this happen? It is because our mind has been intoxicated with greed, anger and ignorance, much too much, and their destructive powers are far beyond our imagination. Therefore, for the cure to be of a fundamental nature, we need to practice how to calm our mind and stay with the moment, by disengaging from all activities, whether good or bad. This process requires lots of patience and perseverance. By looking inwards and retreating from all the good or bad actions of the body, speech and mind, we can experience an extraordinary sense of calmness as our mind is no longer shackled by greed, anger and ignorance. The body is as light as a feather and the mind is as tranquil as the still surface of a lake. This state of mind, this state of meditative concentration is called samatha.

Then, we turn this calm clarity attained from the meditative process to closely and minutely observe the arising of greed, anger and ignorance deeply rooted in and subtly permeating the body and mind. We see that indeed 'everything constantly changes,' we experience firsthand that 'nothing has a fixed, permanent identity' and expose the dualistic absurdity of dividing 'this' from 'that.' We reveal how the mind has been in the clutches of this insane notion of 'I' and 'mine' and discover the powerful drive that grips the mind to expand the territories of 'I' and 'mine.' We see how our anger is aroused when our ambitions are frustrated, and that all depression, grief, worries and distresses are directly caused by the three poisons of greed, anger and ignorance. When we observe and experience reality as it is beyond the shadow of doubt, all mental woes will melt away without trace and only then will our mind be fully restored to its natural state. Knowing this directly is called wisdom or vipassana.

After Sakyamuni Buddha entered parinirvana, his teachings were widely spread among different regions and races. The teachings took on the various cultures, philosophies and religions on the way, and have been passed onto the current generation as living breathing principles.

In the course of dissemination, the Buddha's teachings have been re-arranged and presented in diverse practice systems to best serve the prevailing conditions and particular needs of the people. However, the core of the teachings, sila, samatha and vipassana, have been maintained, unaltered and unchanged for well over two millennia.

Korean Buddhism is no exception. During its 1,700 some years of history, it has developed a wide array of practice methodologies involving Ganhwa Seon meditation, silent illumination meditation, recitation of the Buddha's names, mantras, sutra study, sutra copying and bowing. Any attempt to determine which method is best, however, would be sadly misguided. The Buddha often likened himself to a doctor, using the metaphor of a make-shift raft for river crossing to describe his teachings. A hundred diseases have as many medicines and it would be most unwise to insist only one medicine for the treatment of a wide assortment of ailments.

Korean Buddhism so far has enriched itself by adapting to a multitude of different practices and sutras. However, it has always been faithful to the Mahayana goal of achieving Buddha nature for the benefit of all beings, and all its methodologies have been consistently directed to the cultivation of moral conduct, meditative concentration and wisdom. Furthermore, the success of any practice is always reflected and measured by the depth of wisdom and compassion the practitioner attains. No matter what medicine or treatment the doctor prescribes, they all have the same goal of removing harmful toxins from the patient's system and protecting the healthy cells, designed to fully restore the health of the patient.

61
62
63
64
65

67
68
69
70
71
72

The Essence
of the Korean Buddhist
Practices

01

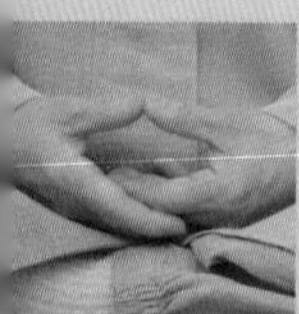

Ganhwa Seon Practice

What is Ganhwa Seon?

'Gan' in Ganhwa means 'to observe,' and 'hwa' the words of the Buddha and Patriarchs. Seon ■ is a transliteration of dhyana and it refers to the East Asian meditation practice by which a practitioner undertakes samatha and vipassana simultaneously. In Ganhwa Seon practice, one contemplates short phrases or the flashes of spontaneous acts displayed by the Buddha or Patriarchs in order to attain full liberation and complete enlightenment from all defilements and delusions.

The Buddha's teachings may seem irritatingly confusing; they appear to go bluntly against our embedded common sense. For instance, we know no other way but perceiving the world around us in terms of "I see," "I hear," "I feel," or "I think." Deeply ingrained in us is the habit of identifying with "I" as an agent who independently experiences sights, sounds, feelings and thoughts. However, the Buddha says, "There is no 'I' that sees, hears, feels or thinks. What is being perceived is no more substantial than figures in a dream, mirages in the desert, and echoes in the valley or shadows cast by people."

The Buddha spent his entire life preaching this observation, which may be construed as an eccentric, even specious or spurious argument. He crisscrossed the Indian sub-continent barefoot, exhorting everyone he met on the path to awaken to this truth. Why did he do that? 'I,' the concept of a permanent self is the result of false impressions formed in the realm of ignorance and illusion, which are the primordial root of all suffering. There is no rest from the never-ending suffering of samsaric cycle of life and death unless we find the way to resolve our delusions.

■

Seon, Chan, Zen

This particular school of Buddhist meditation is represented by the Chinese character 禪 throughout East Asia but read differently as Chan, Seon and Zen in China, Korea and Japan respectively.

It is not easy to comprehend and accept the truth of his words, much less experience it, because we have clung to these misconceptions for too long, enthroning them on the pedestal of common sense. Therefore, we need to momentarily put a pause to miscellaneous thoughts and jumbled emotions subject to the machination of the common sense that has dictated our life so far. Let all your past memories pass by like a silently flowing river, and let all experiences of this moment come and go, in the keen awareness of the transitory nature of all compound structures. As we let them be, we would find that our mind has somehow become far more transparent and lucid. When we are no longer overrun by the thoughts and emotions beholden to the acquired experiences and knowledge, our mind would be as calm as a lake and as clear as a mirror. This state of mind is called samatha. Applying this mirror-like state of mind to reflect the Buddha's teachings, so as to truly understand his words, welcome them into our lives and embody the insight is called vipassana. When the twin wheels of samatha and vipassana are functioning perfectly, we will be set free from the solid walls of our imprisoning thoughts and the quagmire of our sucking emotions. The wisdom will radiate from the mind like a sun, transforming the mind into a beautiful lotus emanating a sweet scent. This is called enlightenment.

No matter how often and how thoroughly we read, listen to and memorize the Buddha's words, without the support of the twin wings of samatha and vipassana, it is nothing but amassing superfluous knowledge. It will not deliver us from suffering or make us happy. Rather, it will be yet another fetter of fabricated concepts that weighs us down. If you are earnest in your quest for liberation, contemplate deeply the words and deeds of the awakened teachers, as reflected through the well-polished lenses of samatha and vipassana, so as to utterly understand 'why did they say it' or 'why did they do it' beyond any shadow of doubt. This process of cultivating samatha and vipassana, the intense exploration of the enlightened teachers' speech and action acutely at odds with common sense, and the sincere probing of the insight behind 'why'—this is Ganhwa Seon.

▪ Ganhwa Seon Practice, Bongeun-sa Temple

Establishment of Ganhwa Seon

Ganhwa Seon is a uniquely Chinese tradition of meditational practice but it still originated directly from the mind of the Buddha. The *Da fantianwangwenfojueyijing* (*"Sutra of the Great King of the Brahman-heaven Inquiring of the Buddha and Resolving His Doubts"*) conveys the account of how Seon came to pass.

The Maha-brahnam, or the Great King of the Brahman-heaven, asked the Buddha at the Dharma assembly at Vulture Peak, "The Bhagavan ("One Revered by the World") has in infinite kindness instructed us for the past 45 years. We can never truly understand how indescribably invaluable your teachings are. Still, I beseech you to graciously bestow us with your teachings on behalf of the beings in all realms, people on earth and gods in heaven."

The Maha-brahnam offered a thousand-petaled golden lotus to the Buddha and turned his own body into the pedestal, and implored the Buddha to elucidate sentient beings

Ascending on the pedestal, the Buddha simply held up the lotus flower. No one in the huge congregation of humans and heavenly beings understood the profundity of this gesture and kept quiet. Only Mahakasyapa cracked his face in a faint smile, stood up and bowed to the Buddha.

Seeing this, the Buddha addressed Mahakasyapa, "I possess the true Dharma eye, the marvelous mind of nirvana, the true form of the formless, the subtle dharma gate that does not rest on words or letters

but is a special transmission outside of the scriptures. This I entrust to Mahakasyapa, who is assured of enlightenment by the conferral of all future Buddhas."

Mahakasyapa was not one of the disciples who always stayed at close attendance to the Buddha. Nor was he much exposed to the Buddha's oral teachings. He was a lone hermit foremost in ascetic practices living in the wilderness. But he was the one who understood the Buddha's purport and therefore worthy to be his successor. According to the *Jingde chuandenglu* (the *Transmission of the Lamp*) and other scriptures, Bodhidharma (?~528), the 28th patriarch in the line of descent from Mahakasyapa, brought to China Mahakasyapa's Seon method of attaining the perfect wisdom by contemplating the Buddha's short expressions or gestures.

Arriving in China in 520, Bodhidharma criticized contemporary Chinese Buddhists for caring only for the accumulation of merits and intellectual studies of doctrines. Instead, he emphasized the key to Buddhism lied in directly experiencing and attaining awakening. He did not rely on theoretical learning, and led his disciples to point directly to their mind and see into the true nature, thus attaining Buddhahood. His teachings infused a breath of fresh air into the Chinese Buddhist teachings of that time, which was too much attached to scholastic pursuit. Eventually, his followers founded Chinese Chan School.

Bodhidharma's Chan was transmitted down the line of Chinese

Patriarchs, to his Dharma heir and 2nd Patriarch Huike (487~593), the 3rd Patriarch Sengcan (?~606), the 4th Patriarch Daoxin (580~651), and the 5th Patriarch Hongren (601~674). The 6th Patriarch Huineng (638~713), the most influential figure in the entire tradition, ushered in the great flowering of Chan. He taught that there is no discrimination between the actual functions of the ordinary mind and the mind of the Buddha, and urged Chan practitioners to directly perceive the original nature that is marked with emptiness. Emptiness that is neither produced or destroyed, neither discriminating between 'I' or 'you,' neither right or wrong, neither good or evil. Huineng preached that seeing this would lead immediately to awakening to the true nature, achieving sudden enlightenment.

Huineng's philosophy of 'mind is the Buddha' was transmitted to Mazu Daoyi (709~788) and Shitou Xiqian (700~790) who opened a new era that witnessed a full expression of Chan practitioners' great capacity and functioning by renowned Chan masters such as Weishan Lingyu (771~853), Linji Yixuan (?~867), Dongshan Liangjie (807~869), Yunmen Wenyan (?~949) and Fayan Wenyi (885~958). These 5 esteemed masters are the ancestors of the lineages called the Five Houses of Chan that became most prominent in China, namely Guiyang, Linji, Caodong, Yunmen and Fayan.

However, several injudicious traits emerged within Chan Schools in the 12th century. Many practitioners hoarded the words of Patriarchs and Chan masters and made free use of their intellectual and discriminatory faculties to contemplate on them, neglecting adequate samatha and vipassana training. Furthermore, they competed to prove their literary superiority by composing clever poems to express their pedantic interpretation. This went squarely against the spirit of Chan that is characterized by "direct insight into the Buddha's teachings not relying upon words and letters." Some Chan practitioners were making a hollow sham of sitting meditation, as a fierce resolve to achieve awakening and the arduous self-check were no longer paramount to their practice. It was against this backdrop that Dahui Zonggao (1089~1163) of the Linji School of Chan founded Ganhwa Seon.

Dahui pointed out that one could not make his or her belly full by the cake in the picture. No matter how well one memorizes or comments on scriptures, it would do little good without taming of mind (samatha) and gaining of wisdom (vipassana). Patriarchs' words would have no benefit without a direct experience of awakening. He was also critical of samatha oriented meditation practices that focus only on suppressing and perishing all mental phenomena of emotions and thoughts, only to become like burned out ashes or desiccated trees. To develop calm abiding and insight in tandem, he recommended investigation of hwadu, literally meaning 'head word', which is a short phrase from the quotations by Patriarchs or Seon teachers. The core of Chan transmission that passed down the line of Mahakasyapa, Bodhidharma, and Huineng was exquisitely and peerlessly embodied by Ganhwa Seon, which spread across China and later Korea where its lineage in a pure form has been excellently preserved to this date.

下心
默言

History of Ganhwa Seon in Korea

▪ Silsang-sa Temple

The Seon lineage of Bodhidharma and Huineng was first introduced to the Korean Peninsula during the Silla period. Eminent Silla monks traveled to Tang China to learn directly under the tutelage of enlightened Chinese masters, and when they returned to Silla, they opened monasteries throughout the peninsula, eventually forming the Nine Mountain Schools of Korean Seon. According to the *Seonmunjosa yechammun* (*the Text for Ceremonies and Contrition Rituals*), the Nine Schools and their founders are as follows:

The Gaji-san school, by Doeui
The Sagul-san school, by Beomil (810~889)
The Saja-san school, by Doyun (798~868)
The Seongju-san school, by Muyeom
The Bongnim-san school, by Hyeonuk (787~869)
The Huiyang-san school, by Doheon (824~882)
The Dongni-san school, by Hyeochoel (785~861)
The Sumi-san school, Ieom(870~936)
The Silsang-san school, by Hongcheok

The Nine Mountain Schools played a critical role in firmly establishing Seon in the Goryeo Dynasty as a leading tradition and collectively reached their pinnacle at the time of Bojo Jinul (1158~1210). Jinul attained his enlightenment while contemplating on a passage from the *Dahuiyulu* (*The Collected Words of Dahui*) at the age of 41 at Sangmuju-am Hermitage in

Mt. Jiri.

Jingak Hyesim (1178~1234), the most eminent disciple of Jinul, popularized the hwadu method and composed the *Seonmun yeomsong*, a massive collection of edifying gongans (koans) selected from a wide range of Buddhist literature. His lineage and teachings were passed on to the 16 National Preceptors of Suseonsa Society.

Taego Bou (1301~1382), Naong Hyegeun (1320~1376) and Baekun Gyeonghan (1299~1374) securely established Ganhwa Seon as a definitive method for the Korean Seon tradition. Direct transmission and affirmation of one's enlightenment experience by the enlightened teacher is considered the most important milestone of one's monastic career above all else in the Seon tradition. These 3 masters, contemporaries and colleagues to each other, all went to China and received transmission from authentic Chan lineage holders.

Taego Bou practiced for 20 years with bone-grinding exertion to achieve spiritual awakening and reached a constant state of awareness uninterrupted while awake or asleep at 37, and finally at the age of 38 attained enlightenment. He went over Yuan China to have his experience validated by a teacher and received a transmission from Shiwu Qinggong (1272~1352), a renowned master of the Linji sect who bestowed Bou with a *kasaya* (ceremonial robe) and a staff as tokens of his credentials.

Naong Hyegeun is known to have reached enlightenment at the age of 27. He studied for 10 years in China under the esteemed Linji Chan master Pingshan Chulin (1279~1361) and received the ceremonial robe and whisk as tokens of transmission. He was also a student of the Indian master Shikong who presented Naong with the ceremonial robe, whisk and the transmission document written in Sanskrit.

Baekun Gyeonghan entered monastic life at a fairly young age, and also went to China and received transmission from Shiwu Qinggong. Baekun edited and compiled the *Gikjisimcheyojeo*, the oldest extant printed material in the world produced by metal movable types.

The Dharma descendents of Taego Bou have carried his Seon lineage down to the present, still flourishing today, through the succession of such masters as Hwanam Honsu (1320~1392), Gugok Kakun, Byeokgye Jeongsim, Byeoksong Jieom (1464~1534) and Buyong Yeonggwan (1485 ~1571).

Cheongheo Hyujeong (1520~1604) and Buhyu Seonsu (1543~1615), Yeonggwan's designated Dharma heirs, gave rise to 2 major strands of Seon at that time. Among the disciples of Cheongheo Hyujeong, Samyeong Yujeong (1544~1610) and Pyeonyang Eongi (1581~1644) rose to noble prominence and the latter became the ancestor of a thriving lineage still existing to this date.

In modern Korea, Geongheo Seongu (1849~1912) and Yongseong Jinjong (1864~1940) revitalized hwadu practice, bringing in the renaissance of a new era of Ganhwa Seon, which is the representative Buddhist practice system widely in use today.

Ganhwa Seon practice Today

Institutions committed to Ganhwa Seon training are called Seon centers. Seon centers can be roughly divided into 2 kinds, depending on whether they allow the laity to join or not.

There are approximately 100 Seon centers which are exclusively for monastics. Over 2,000 monks and nuns participate in meditation retreats ("tranquil shelter") twice a year in the summer and the winter. It is a period of intensified practice during which uninterrupted residence is mandatory. Registered monks and nuns isolate themselves behind the gate of the Seon center for 3 months, bound by the vigorous regulations called *the Rules of Purity* that strictly govern the conduct of the retreat community. During the retreat, individualistic behavior is not condoned. Monks and nuns in training wake up at 2~3 am at dawn and go to bed around 9~10 pm. The daily retreat routine consists of morning and evening services, meals and communal work sessions but the participants dedicate most of their time to the sessions of intense sitting meditation. Some days are specially set aside for 'ferocious effort' during which sleep is not allowed to make room for round-the-clock sitting meditation.

There are a great number of Seon centers open to the general public all over Korea. They are operated quite differently compared to the monastic Seon centers. Laypeople are not required to engage in communal life and can join only for the meditation sessions. Their *Rules of Purity* are not as stringent, and lay retreats are not necessarily 3 months either, and participants are given flexibility to adjust the period. Well known Seon centers running Ganhwa Seon programs for laypeople are: Ankuk Zen Center, Geumgang Seon Center, Wonmyeong Seon Center, Bongeun-sa Temple, Gongsaeng Seon Center, Yukjo-sa Temple, MitaSeon Center and Odeung Seon Center. Many illustrious Temples, centers and institutes also offer various Ganhwa Seon based meditation classes, such as Bulgwang-sa Temple, Mihwang-sa Temple, Geumsan-sa Temple and Beomeo-sa Temple to name a few.

Ankuk Zen Center has centers in Busan, Seoul and other cities in Korea. Their program structure comprises 'programs for beginners' and 'programs for pledged members.' Beginners attend Dharma teachings to arouse bodhi mind, i.e., aspiration to attain Buddhahood and save all beings, and learn how to take up a hwadu. To become a member, one must complete the beginners' program, register with the members' association, attend regular Dharma Assemblies and join meditation groups. Only pledged members can participate in retreats.

Geumgang Seon Center is located in Gaepo-dong, Seoul, offering classes on the Buddhist scriptures, Dharma talks and Ganhwa Seon meditation classes. Ganhwa Seon meditation classes are divided into Meditation for Beginners, Jeongsu Group, Meditation for Middle & High School Students and Meditation for College Students. Those who finish Meditation for Beginners are qualified to join Jeongsu Group, which meets once a week for the group practice.

Bongeun-sa Temple is in Samsung-dong, Seoul. It receives membership applications for a one-month lay retreat, during which participating members are immersed in Ganhwa Seon practice from 4am to 9pm and have a interview with the Dharma teacher every Saturday to talk about issues and experiences arising during meditation.

The Jogye Order of Korean Buddhism has developed ‘Ganhwa Seon Program for Beginners’ in 2005 and the Lay Buddhist Association and the Social Welfare Foundation of the Jogye Order offer courses based on this program.

1 2
3

1. Ankuk Zen Center
2. Bongeun-sa Temple
3. Geumgang Seon Center

Characteristics of Ganhwa Seon

Ganhwa Seon, as mentioned before, has consummately espoused Bodhidharma and Huineng's wisdom, heart and soul. The characteristics of Ganhwa Seon are indeed those of Seon in general. There are a couple of features of Seon that stand out when compared to other Buddhist practices.

Foremost in Seon is that all beings are originally the Buddha. Seon masters say, "You are the Buddha. You are not this being that is perceived to be born, age, ail and die. You are inherently unsullied by suffering, carefree and dignified. You just cannot believe in it, that you are already the Buddha."

This is one of the famous gathas, or the verses, on the *Diamond Sutra* by Yefu:

Wide and open path
Bright and clear
Inherent to every being
Already perfect

Chan master Huangbo (?~850) said in his *Wanlinglu*:

"The mind of sentient beings is the Buddha as it is. From all the Buddhas of ten directions down to the squirming worms, inherent to all is the Buddha nature. Therefore, Bodhidharma deigned to come from the west to teach only one Dharma, that of one mind, pointing to the truth that all sentient beings are already the Buddha. It is not something to be achieved by effort. Directly point to your mind and see your true nature. That, and only that. There is nothing to gain or to be gained."

Seon tradition emphasizes the sudden awakening. The cave immersed in darkness for several millennia is illuminated immediately upon the lighting of a single candle. If we are shown directly to our true nature by a word conferred by a sage, then we are the Buddha. There is no need to endure a lengthy practice to see this to become a free and wise being like the Buddha. This is described as "leaping in to the realm of the Tathagata and enter it at once." Seon is primarily about the experience of awakening, not so much about practice, attested by the words and actions of Patriarchs contained in Seon histories and their discourse records. It is well exemplified by the exchange between Huike and Bodhidharma.

Huike inquired of his teacher Bodhidharma one day, "My mind is still agitated. Please comfort my mind." Bodhidharma answered, "Bring your mind to me. I will sooth it." Huike deeply reflected on this for a long time and said, "I cannot find my mind, no matter how hard I try." Bodhidharma said, "I have already calmed your mind." Upon this, Huike underwent a complete awakening, rejoicing in the ultimate freedom from all sufferings.

Chan schools regard the awakened mind of Patriarchs and that of the Buddha as one and the same. Therefore, the speech and deed of Patriarchs are as sacred and revered as those of the Buddha. For instance, the *Platform Sutra*, the collected words of the 6th Patriarch Huineng is referred to as a 'sutra,' the title reserved to describe the discourses of Sakyamuni Buddha himself. Hence, direct guidance from the enlightened teacher is most intrinsic to the attainment of enlightenment, which must

be verified by a qualified master. No matter how wise and unhindered one appears, it is considered of no consequence without such approval by a teacher. The *Taegohwasang eorok* (*The Collected Words of Taego*) states:

"Once you reach that state, you will find that your ignorance has been shattered away before you know it. After you undergo such an awakening experience, please make sure to receive a conferral from the enlightened teacher. Without proper audience and approval from such a teacher, All 10 out of 10 seekers of enlightenment will turn out to be maras without fail. I sincerely beseech you to be oh-so-careful."

Embodied insight and live experience cultivated through extensive samatha and vipassana training are the priority in Seon. Covetous pursuit and acquisition of knowledge is strongly discouraged. Therefore, unless you are awakened, you are not permitted to repeat your teacher's words; even reading and memorizing Buddha's words could sometimes be frowned upon. Following is a story from the *Dunwurudaoyaomenlun* ("The *Collected Words of Dazhu Huihai*").

A disciple of Dazhu Huihai asked one day, "Why am I forbidden to memorize the sutras? Why is it that the sutras are someone else's words?" Dazhu Huihai replied, "Parrots may mimic human speech without truly understanding the meaning. Sutras are tools to convey the meaning of the Buddha's teaching. Memorizing without understanding is just mimicking the sounds of his words. This is why."

What is Hwadu?

'Hwadu' literally means a head word or head story. But it is not the words from our mundane dialogues, which are made up with concepts and set in the mould of common sense. Then, what is the hwadu? It is the words and actions of the Buddha and Patriarchs, which are often absurdly incongruent with our common sense. Let's take an example.

A monk asked Yunmen Wenyan.
"What is the Buddha?"
Yunmen Wenyan answered.
"Dried shit on the stick."

Buddhists worship the Buddha as the flawlessly pure, immeasurably wise and infinitely compassionate saint, probably the most irresistibly attractive being that ever graced this earth. Most Buddhists think this way without really questioning their thoughts. However, Yunmen declared that the Buddha is nasty, foul, stinking and revolting 'dried shit on the stick.' How would you feel if we heard it directly from him? If you are a Buddhist, it would be considerably baffling, even upsetting. Where does this feeling of disconcertment come from? It derives from the clash with our common sense and experiences filtered through our discriminative thinking.

When we hear something so sharply at odds with what we think we know for sure, there are two possible reactions. We cry, "It is completely outrageous!" and turn our back on it. Or, we stop and ask: "Why did he say such a strange thing?" In the former, we trust our experience and thinking more than the speaker; in the latter, we trust the speaker more than our own knowledge.

If we had gotten to know him well, seen how excruciatingly assiduous his training has been, how unaffectedly genuine and sincere he was, how astute and wise his judgment was, and if we had seen his unflaggingly kind and gentle spirit permeating his daily life, we would have trusted that he would not have wasted his breath in frivolous nonsense and asked ourselves, "Why on earth did he describe our sacred Lord Buddha as 'dried shit on the stick?'… Why?"

This is hwadu. If you are not a Buddhist, such a question may not last long: "Who cares whether the Buddha is a dried shit or a chunk of gold?" You may readily give up the roused question and cheerfully return to the world of fabricated concepts that we call common sense. However, if you are a pious Buddhist, and if you have been trying all your life to emulate the saintly example of the Buddha, and if you trust Yunmen as a fully enlightened master, his gripingly short answer can shake your whole world. Suddenly flung into the irreconcilable chasm created by the clash between 'Our Holy Lord Buddha' and Yunmen's 'dried shit on the stick,' you are unable to choose and overcome with the question: "The Buddha is 'dried shit on the stick?!What on earth does that mean?"

To resolve this riddle, you may seek to find a compromise somewhere in between your intellectual conceptualization and Yunmen's words: "Yes, the scriptures say that the true nature is neither sacred nor mundane, clean nor dirty, or noble nor vulgar. Everything is innately equal. That must be why the Master equated the Buddha with the dried shit."

However, you would start criticize your own compromise before long: "However, if there is no sacredness or banality in the first place, why do the words "sacred" or "banal" exist at all? If there is indeed not even a hair's breadth of difference between them, why not use just one word? Why use two opposing words? Also, if 'sacred' has the same meaning with 'dirty,' does that imply that I can say 'dirty Buddha' and 'sacred shit?"

A few scant words from Yunmen raised a big question in you. You try to formulate an answer, and then discover holes in it, reject it and subsequently seek another compromise. This new compromise would again be exposed as faulty and you go after yet another answer. This can go on and on. As the question grows bigger and bigger, it drives away from your mind other matters or interests. As you keep dismissing answers you suggest, your accustomed trust in your familiar logic and thinking diminishes. As this process repeats itself, before you know it, only one big mass of questioning suffuses the mind: "Why on earth did he say the Buddha is 'dried shit on the stick?'… Why?"

All contemplation relying on pre-existing concepts and logics is frustrated and exhausted. Only the mass of questioning persists, searing the mind like a burning lump of coal. Only investigating this 'one head word' that completely entraps your mind on the foundation of samatha and vipassana—this is Ganhwa Seon practice.

How to Practice Ganhwa Seon?

Methodology

Seon underscores the role of an enlightened teacher more than anything else. If you are interested in Ganhwa Seon practice, the most effective and direct path is to find an enlightened teacher who would upset our common sense topsy-turvy and turn all our experiences and knowledge to dust with a single blow. It would be truly a blessing to meet such a being, receive a hwadu, have this teacher check your progress and verify spiritual experiences.

If such an opportunity does not manifest itself, the use of a gongan, or more commonly known as koan in the West, is recommended. Gongans are the compiled list of hwadus applied and verified by the generations of Patriarchs. Peruse gongans contained in the prime examples of the edited collections such as the *Chuandenglu* (the *Record of the Transmission of the Lamp*, containing 1,700 gongans), the *Biyanlu* (*the Blue Cliff Record*, 100 gongans), the *Congronglu* (the *Congrong Hermitage Record*, 100 gongans) or the *Wumen guan* (the *Gateless Barrier*, 48 gongans) and choose one that sets your mind on fire with the burning sense of questioning. Once a hwadu is selected, the question roused by the hwadu has to be tackled. This is called investigating a hwadu. Investigating a hwadu presupposes three firmly established frames of mind.

First is a steadfast faith. This means you unwaveringly trust that the Buddha or the enlightened teacher who offers their speech or deed as hwadu; that they would never have indulged in gibberish babble; and perfect wisdom and liberation from all sufferings will be attainable once this big question is resolved.

Second is a strong resolve. Feel deeply humbled and outraged by the fact that a single word of an enlightened teacher befuddles you so thoroughly. Be passionately courageous and resolute that you will live a life as carefree, dignified and liberated as that of the Buddha and Patriarchs by getting to the bottom of the big question.

Third is a big doubt. Without a big doubt, it is difficult to be raptly immersed in the hwadu. Investigate a hwadu like a cat pursuing a mouse, a hen brooding eggs, or a man hanging from a cliff by a single rope. Intense concentration can only be drawn on such a big doubt.

Unless these three conditions are devotedly fulfilled, investigation of the hwadu would be unlikely to come to fruition, not to mention bring any benefits.

Once a hwadu is chosen, and all the conditions are carried satisfactorily through, now is the time to get to boring into the hwadu. Investigating the hwadu can be done 24 hours a day, whether you are standing up, sitting down, walking around or lying down, but still the most effective way is to calm your mind and enter samadhi, or dhyana, through sitting meditation. Instructions on the recommended steps for the sitting meditation are as follows:

• Select a spot. Choose as quiet and clean a place as possible. Try to avoid where it is too cold or hot.
• Sit on the floor. Use two cushions, one to spread out on the floor, and the other to be folded in half and placed on top of the first. Sit perched on top of the folded cushion. Cross the legs. Put the right foot onto the left thigh and then lift the left foot and place it onto the right thigh, forming an X shape with the calves. It would be better if both knees touch the ground. This is called a full lotus position. If sitting in the full lotus position is uncomfortable or painful, choose the half lotus position instead, with one foot resting on the other thigh. At most Seon centers, sitting is donc in a half lotus. If the half lotus position still causes physical pain or discomfort, it is okay to sit on the chair with the spine straightened up.
• Straighten up the spine and relax the shoulders by lightly swinging the torso left and right.

• Put your hands on top of each other, with both palms up, and rest them lightly near the navel. When the left foot is underneath the right, the left palm is below as well. If the right foot is on top, so is the hand. Lift and touch the thumbs to form a rough circle. If this feels awkward, resting the hands on each knee is also fine.
• Relax all the muscles in the body and ease the breathing. Make sure though that relaxation would not result in back bending. Eyes are half closed and look downward. Breathe naturally and easily.
• Investigate the hwadu.
• Meditate 30 minutes to one hour, or for the pre-set amount of time.
• When the time is up, slowly uncross the legs, stand up and walk around for a bit in silence. When drowsiness, physical pain or a headache becomes too overwhelming, it is all right to leave the cushion and walk around the vicinity for awhile.

▪ Ganhwa Seon Practice, Bongeun-sa Temple

Benefits

If the hwadu is penetrated through by Ganhwa Seon practice, a complete enlightenment perfectly equaling that of the Buddha will be attained. Dahui Zonggao wrote in his *Shuzhuang*, "When a being achieves complete enlightenment, its heart shines radiantly from inside as if 100,000 suns and moons light up simultaneously, and the mind fathoms all the worlds of the ten directions at one glance, and is free of all fabricated concepts and thoughts."

When the hwadu is penetrated, that is, if the question that helplessly and utterly binding the mind clears up without a single spot of doubt left behind, the capabilities of the Buddha himself will fully manifest in you. There is only the perfect wisdom of the Buddha and absolute freedom from delusions and ignorance, no longer haunted and tormented by anger and greed. This ultimate state becomes you. No. You do not become anything. You just realize at long last that you are this all this time, you always have been, and inherently so.

Even if we do not reach this blissful state any time soon, genuine practice of Ganhwa Seon can bring about many edifying experiences.

- Concentration comes easier, strong and sound.
- One is not as sensitively reacting to or easily swayed by external stimulus.
- One does not get as readily excited or depressed.
- One is no longer as impatient and compelled to achieve or possess something.
- One finds oneself observing the vicissitude of emotions from one step away.
- One no longer argues one's points as frantically.
- The dualistic boundaries dividing I and other, this and that, or right and wrong crumble and blur.
- Body and mind are much more at ease and peace whoever one meets, wherever one is and whatever one does.
- It is of course clear that everything compounds and disperses according to the law of cause and effect.

Musing From a Guide

Master Seolbong abruptly blurted to any disciple who came seeking his audience, "What is this?"
So, what is this?
What is this that sits down, stands up, walks about and lies down?
What is this that sees, hears, smells, tastes, feels and thinks?
What is this that eats, works, speaks and sleeps?
What is this that has been born, ages, ails and dies?
What is this that likes this and dislikes that, that loves this person and hates that person?
What on earth is this that rejoices when it possesses what it likes, and grieves over the loss of it?
The answer is all too often and too quickly 'I.'
Please take this 'I' out in the open so that I can see it.
We all say so easily "I am sad" or "I am happy."
Does that mean that sadness is you? Or, Happiness is you? Or, both sadness and happiness are you? Or, neither sadness nor happiness is you?

If sadness is definitely you, you would be sad for the rest of your life. If happiness is you, you would be happy for the rest of your life. However, the moment of sadness does not last forever, neither does the moment of happiness. So, what are you?

If both sadness and happiness are you, why should you be so adverse about being sad and so ecstatic about being happy? If indeed both sadness and happiness are equally you, perhaps the moments of joy are no more special than the moments of sorrow, therefore there is no more need for laughs or tears. Is it really so?

If neither sadness nor happiness is you, then you are a being that has nothing to do with either sorrow or joy. Then you cannot really say "I am sad" or "I am happy." Is it really your case?

Does it sound like sophist double talk? If not, please reflect on it.

I am not asking some brilliantly clever riposte.

The only thing I am encouraging you to do is ask yourself,

"What is this?"

The Essence
of the Korean Buddhist
Practices

02

Yeombul, or Buddha-recitation Practice

What is *Yeombul*, or Buddha-recitation?

Yeombul is the practice of reciting or recollecting the names of the Buddha. It is a translation of the term *buddhanusmti* or *buddhasati*, which means Buddha contemplation or Buddha invocation.

Why do we think of the Buddha at all? Every one of us at some point in our lives has mimicked the hairdo or fashion style of our favorite stars. If we interact with or think of a person often enough, our own actions and thoughts start to echo those of the person. If we invoke the Buddha often enough in our mind, before we know it, we would be as composed in action, as gentle in speech and as calm and exact in thoughts as the Buddha. All Buddhas have made a solemn vow that "all living beings shall revel in the same joy and peace as I do." If we have our mind etched with their names and the thought of them, the power vested in their vows eliminates suffering from our mind and makes peace and wisdom flow. *Yeombul* is a practice by which one conquers all sufferings and attains ultimate bliss by ardently invoking and chanting the names of Buddhas and Bodhisattvas.

Korean Buddhism follows the Mahayana tradition. Mahayana Buddhism does not claim that Sakyamuni Buddha is the only one. Korean Buddhists believe that innumerous Buddhas have preceded the historical Buddha, who will be succeeded by countless future Buddhas. A legion of contemporary Buddhas are currently scattered all over the universe busy saving all living creatures. Furthermore, myriad of Bodhisattvas, who outnumber the Buddhas by tens of thousands, are helping people in all quarters by practicing the six paramitas of generosity (dana), morality (sila), forbearance (ksanti), effort (virya), meditation (dhyana) and wisdom (prajna).

Yeombul practice can be categorized depending on to whom the homage is dedicated. Different Buddhas and Bodhisattvas appeal to different individuals and times. Some of the Buddhas and Bodhisattvas in which the generations of Korean *yeombul* practitioners have sought refuge are: Sakyamuni, Amitabha, Maitreya, Aksobhya, Bhaisajyaguru-vaidurya, Avalokitesvara and Ksitigarbha.

Situations that are completely beyond our control unavoidably happen to all of us. We fall prey to sudden illnesses, or are caught in hapless accidents. We are ambushed by an abrupt loss of something or someone dear to us. Achievements of a lifetime go up in smoke. Sometimes, we are face-to-face with death, suddenly staring right into its eyes. When our backs are despairingly to the wall, it is virtually impossible to think and react with calm poise and cool reason. Except for a rare few who have attained deep samadhi and unshakable prajna, we sink into the bottomless pit of sorrow or wail in abysmal fear. However, bitter tears and frantic clamoring would not solve the problem; they just invite even more grief and greater panic.

If this happens, call upon the Buddha and Bodhisattvas. They take an oath that "I shall remove all traces of torment and fear from all sentient beings." If you are sincere and earnest, they will answer our call without fail. They will end the reign of terror and heal the tears inside of you and put the smile of a Buddha on your lips.

Doctrinal *Ground*

- Avalokitesvara Bodhisattva carved in stone, Gilsang-sa Temple

Nagarjuna, in his *Dasabhumika-vibhasa* (the *Commentary on the Sutra of Ten Bodhisattva Stages*), wrote:

"Just as there are rugged roads and easy, smooth roads, the path over the sea of Dharma can be either crooked and perilous or even and straight. Imagine you are going to a far, faraway place. If you have to walk all the way, it would be really tiring. But if you are on board a seafaring vessel, it can be a fun, comfortable journey. Likewise, to reach the land of bliss, one can cross the sea of Dharma by ardent rigor and toil or glide through the sea on a vessel propelled onward by the power of faith."

The easy way to the land of bliss is *yeombul* practice of reciting the names of the Buddha. Nagarjuna says, "By invoking the names of the Buddha, one can make all afflictions and negative karmas of the past go away and gain perfect wisdom." How is it possible? It is because of the pledges the Buddha and Bodhisattvas make while devoting their lives during the countless ages to the Bodhisattva acts.

Amitabha Buddha erected the pristine, exquisite and magnificent Buddha Land free from all mundane suffering. He vowed to grant rebirth in his realm to anyone who wishes for it, and bestows the perfect wisdom and therefore Buddhahood to all the residents of his land. He also pledged that any being that hears his name would secure the perfect wisdom, even if they dwell in other realms. His paradisiacal territory is called the Pure Land (*Sukhavati*) and located in the West afar. His vow is endowed with such power that even a single utterance of his name, if done with all of one's heart, would hasten the entry into the Western Paradise, dead or alive. A detailed description of Amitabha Buddha's past lives, his vows and the Pure Land of Western Paradise can be found in the *Sutra of Immeasurable Life,* the *Sutra of the Meditation on the Buddha of Immeasurable Life* and the *Amitabha Sutra.*

Maitreya Buddha is destined to appear in this world to be the next Buddha in the future. He received the conferral from Sakyamuni Buddha himself and currently presides over a throng of heavenly beings in the Tusita Heaven. When he finally descends upon this world, he will save the human race from all disasters and distresses with only three rounds of Dharma teachings. Abundant references are made about Maitreya in the *Sutra of Maitreya's Ascension,* the *Sutra on the Descent of Maitreya,* and the *Sutra on the Completion of Maitreya's Reign.*

Avalokitesvara Bodhisattva is acutely attuned to pick up any sound of agony or cries for help. He vowed to rush to help them in any way possible. Therefore, simply recalling his image in mind will expel all fears when one is beset with danger. Avalokitesvara is known for his ability to shape-shift at will, assuming whatever form—Buddhas, Bodhisattvas, gods, men, women or even animals—that is best suited to save each person in dire need. The *Lotus Sutra* carries an entire chapter on Avalokitesvara.

Ksitigarbha Bodhisattva, from time immemorial, has devoted

himself to the vow to "refuse Buddhahood until I deliver all beings who are suffering from the consequences of their sins using no matter what it takes, until the whole universe is devoid of living creatures languishing in pain." Ksitigarbha even braves the fires of hell to save the wicked. The *Sutra on the Past Vows of Ksitigarbha Bodhisattva,* and the *Sutra on the Ten Cakras of Ksitigarbha* contain detailed accounts of this Bodhisattva associated with the dead and the hells.

There are many, many more Mahayana scriptures that record the past lives and vows of the Buddhas and Bodhisattvas. These texts confirm that *yeombul* practice is a proven path leading not only to the deliverance from suffering in this world but also to the perfect enlightenment and absolute bliss.

▪ Stone statue of Maitreya Buddha on the site of Mireuk-sa Temple

History of *Yeombul* Practice in Korean Buddhism

The *Memorabilia of the Three Kingdoms,* a collection of legends, folklores, and historical accounts relating to the ancient three kingdoms of Korea, conveys a poem by a Buddhist monk who was broken hearted over the death of his sister.

> The path of life and death crosses over,
> Oh, my heart is devastated!
> You departed without a word of farewell.
> Like fallen leaves flopping around in the wind,
> In the chilly morning of an autumn day,
> Born of a same branch,
> But no longer together, not even a trace behind.
> My dear, let's meet again in the world of Amitabha.
> Please wait for me. I will do utmost in my practice.

This poem, composed by Wolmyeong, a monk during the time of King Gyeongdeok's reign (?~765), indicates the *yeombul* practice was already widespread in the Silla kingdoms of Korea. The *Memorabilia of the Three Kingdoms* has another story related to the practice of Buddha-recitation.

"There was a female servant named Ukmyeon in the household of a nobleman called Guijin. She was saddled with hard work from dawn to midnight without given a moment of rest but she never let the name of

Amitabha slip from her mind. One day, when she bowed with her palms together and recited the name of Amitabha in a room, the sky suddenly resonated with a grand music. Ukmyeon soared upward, shooting through the roof toward the west. She soon transformed into the Buddha casting off her human body."

Yeombul practice does not require elaborate training or lengthy education. Therefore, it quickly became popular among the common folks of lower classes who barely made it hand to mouth. Wonhyo (617~686) is by far the most broadly respected Buddhist figure who ever lived on the Korean peninsula. Wonhyo disrobed and wore his hair long to go to the people of Silla and wandered the countryside singing and dancing alongside the ignorant peasants and taught them to chant 'Namu Amitabul.' Consequently, the villages and streets of Silla rang with the chanting of 'Namu Amitabul' by the young and old. '*Namu*' is a Chinese transliteration of '*namo*,' which means 'taking refuge.'

Silla monk Baljing established a society dedicated to 10,000 days of *yeombul* practice in the 17th year of King Gyeongdeok's reign (758) at Wongak-sa Temple (currently Geonbong-sa Temple). 1,823 members of the society applied themselves to 30 years of unceasing efforts, and at the conclusion of their practice, 31 of them, including Baljing, flew up into the sky, discarded their human bodies and were reborn in the Western Paradise.

Yeombul was applied not only to earning rebirth in the Buddha

Land and meriting the Buddha's blessings but also as an important practice technique to cultivate wisdom in this world. According to the *Vimalakirti-nirdesa Sutra,* "Clean minds purify the land," and many Seon masters enthusiastically embraced *yeombul* into their practice. Stilling their fragmented thoughts and focusing the mind only on the Buddha, they experienced the defilement-free state of samadhi, and attained the perfect wisdom by observing the true nature of 'I' thinking only of the Buddha. As such, they were able to proclaim, "My mind is Amitabha, so is the paradise," and from the mid Joseon Dynasty, it became customary for Seon monks in later lives to take *yeombul* as their primary practice. Master Naong (1320~1376), one of the most esteemed Seon masters of the Korean Buddhist tradition left a famous gatha regarding *yeombul.*

> Where is Amitabha Buddha?
> Chisel his name in your mind and always dwell on it.
> Reflect, reflect and reflect; when even the reflection is gone,
> Whole body and mind will radiate dazzling golden light.

▪ Geonbong-sa Temple

Yeombul Practice Today

▪ Guin-sa Temple

The practice of *yeombul* has been ubiquitous in Korean Buddhism. Buddhists chanting homage to Buddhas or Bodhisattvas, with palms together or clicking prayer beads as a way of counting, can be commonly sighted at any temple in the country.

Geonbong-sa Temple, Jeongto-sa Temple, Daewon-sa Temple, Dongsanbanya-hoe and Baekryeonjeong-sa Temple are currently accommodating 10,000-day *Yeombul* Societies. Munsasubeop-hoe, Mangyeong-sa Temple, Mahabori-sa Temple and *Yeombul* Seon Center offer regular *yeombul* practice programs. Jeongto-sa Temple located in Seongnam, Gyeonggi-do Province in particular runs parallel classes on the doctrinal teachings on the Pure Land Buddhism. The temple also has a system in place to interview practitioners and provide practice guidelines and counseling based on their experiences. Daewon-sa Temple located in Hwasun operates a 2-day *yeombul* oriented temple stay program on the first and third weekend every month. Mahabori-sa Temple in Bongcheon-dong, Seoul has a 8-day program dedicated to *yeombul* practice.

Master Sangwol (1911~1974), one of the most prominent Seon teachers of modern Korea was also well known for stressing the importance of *yeombul* practice. He said that the adoration of Avalokitesvara releases all beings from the tyranny of calamities and adversities, as it is a vital gateway to the state of deep meditative absorption and awakening of wisdom. His teachings have been received passionately and practiced widely by the public. At Guin-sa Temple founded by Master Sangwol, chanting Avalokitesvara's name is an integral part of training along with communal work and sitting meditation, and the temple runs a training program which lasts 5 days all year round. A one-month retreat is also organized seasonally in the summer and the winter, during which both monastics and laypeople seclude themselves for a period of intense training.

Master Cheonghwa (1924~2003) is another modern teacher who renewed the tradition of *Yeombul* Seon(Seon by way of Buddha-recitation) as a superb method to bear witness to the truth of 'Our mind is the Buddha.' Currently, Seongryun-sa Temple, Gwangryun-sa Temple, Jeongjung-sa Temple, Seongwon-sa Temple and Hyeun-sa Temple are some of the temples that practice *Yoembul* Seon according to his teachings.

How to Practice *Yeombul*?

▪ *Yeombul* Practice, Guin-sa Temple

Methodology

Yeombul can be practiced virtually everywhere, yet it would be more effective to do it at a temple where the Buddha or a bodhisattva to be venerated in *Yeombul* is enshrined. Turning the prayer beads can also help. *Yeombul* can be categorized into 4 practices depending on what the practitioner's mind rests on during *yeombul*.

- **Invoke the name of the Buddha and meditate on him**: find an unoccupied and quiet spot, sit composed, focus the thought only on the Buddha and Bodhisattva chosen as the refuge and repeatedly chant his name. Swirls of dizzying thoughts would settle down, replaced by uninterrupted yearning for the Buddha or Bodhisattva, gently nudging the mind into samadhi by a single pious act.
- **Contemplate on the image of the Buddha and repeat his name**: visualize the image of the Buddha or Bodhisattva on the painting, etch their benevolent visions and keep visiting them in the mind.
- **Observe laksanas (marks of excellence)**: Buddhas are endowed with unique marks and merits, exhibiting 32 bodily characteristics which manifest the perfect wisdom and the state of bliss he achieved. Select one of the 32 marks and observe them attentively.
- **Reflect on the true nature of the Buddha**: the Buddha taught us that what we perceive as fixed reality in a time continuum is in fact groundless attachment stemming from delusion, like a person crying "snake" to a scrap of rope on the road at night. Therefore, realize that what we firmly believe as existing indeed does not exist, and the image of the Buddha is also no exception to this truth. The *Saptasatikaprajnaparamita* says, "The true nature does not appear or disappear, come or go, and it has no name or form.

This is called the Buddha. Observe the true nature of one's own body as well as any Buddhas."

There are three ways of reciting the names of the Buddhas and Bodhisattvas.

- Say their names only in the mind while thinking about them.
- Whisper their names while thinking about them.
- Call out their names loud to the beats of wooden hand-bell or drum.

The recommended procedures for *yeombul* practice are as follows:

- First, bow to pay homage to the Buddha, the savior of all living creatures with infinite loving kindness and compassion.
- Bare to the Buddha or Bodhisattva all past misconducts and mistakes candidly and offer contrition.
- Convey the wish that one wants to be fulfilled by the Buddhas and Bodhisattvas.
- Chant the names of the Buddhas and Bodhisattvas sincerely and ardently wishing that it will come true.
- Practice *yeombul* for one or two hours or for the time set aside.
- Vow to dedicate all the merits accumulated through this practice with all others.

Various postures can be applied to *yeombul* practice. One can stand straight with palms together, kneel, sit in the lotus position, place hands on the knees in the lotus position, bow, walk or go around one's daily routine.

Benefits

Countless exegesises on sutras and various writings of *yeombul* practitioners document the great merits of *yeombul* practice. Some of more illustrative benefits are as follows:

- The Buddha or Bodhisattva appears during *yeombul* or in a dream.
- Practitioner feels a mysterious luminescence encircling him/herself.
- One can actually feel all the past misconducts vanish and liberated from guilt.
- One no longer becomes tense or fearful in a dangerous or urgent situation.
- Mind is calmed and the head is cleared.
- Words of the sages come in a clear understanding.
- Expressions on the face become soft and gentle.
- Help come voluntarily from unexpected corners.
- Undesirable situations are resolved by themselves.
- The body becomes free of illness and healthy.
- Potentials lying dormant inside manifest.
- Lifespan increases.
- The Buddhas and Bodhisattvas become constant guardians.
- The clarity and peace of mind can be maintained even at the moment of dying.
- One can secure a favorable rebirth after death.

▪ *Yeombul* Practice, Jikji-sa Temple

They are not just obscure descriptions from old books. Many *yeombul* practitioners still bear witness vividly to all these merits and benefits even today.

It would be better to tidy up one's body as well as bearings of mind. Clean up, put on fresh clothes, and sweep the surroundings before staring *yeombul* practice. Employ calm attitude to your conduct and avoid speaking unnecessarily as much as possible.

One has to be absolutely sincere in invoking the names of the Buddhas or Bodhisattvas. Such sincerity can be engendered only with the unyielding faith in the Buddha and Bodhisattvas that they will surely help us. But faith is not something that can be summoned at will. It is difficult to trust someone at first sight. Likewise, we have to know well the Buddha or Bodhisattva to whom we are appealing, so it would be more constructive to read or learn beforehand about the lives and vows of the Buddha or Bodhisattva we choose as our refuge.

It is also crucial to be very clear what we truly want. If we do not know for certain why we are praying to the Buddha or Bodhisattva, we cannot really muster sincerity or enthusiasm necessary to induce positive changes. *Yeombul* can be practiced ideally 24/7, for the duration of our entire lives. If this is not possible, however, then being regular about it is recommended for fuller benefits. For example, set certain periods and totally immerse in the practice, like 3 days, 7 days, 30 days or 100 days. Or incorporate it into one's daily routine, like one or two hours a day, or 108, 1,000 or 10,000 times of recitation.

Musing From a Guide

Set your mind on the Buddha and Bodhisattva all the time, and gently whisper their names.
If you are walking in contemplation of him, he would be in your steps.
If you speak with him in your thought, he would sooth and soften your words.
If you work with his presence in your mind, everyone around you would be praising your achievement before you know it.
If you fall asleep while thinking of him, you would meet him and have a warm, heart-to-heart talk in your dream.
If you wake up cherishing his name, a joyful day would await you in the morning.
If you call upon his name, he would wash away all the grief and anger weighing down your heart like a squall.
If you think of him, he would show you beyond any shadow of doubt that those who drive you insanely outraged, worried sick or forlornly sad are in fact just as insubstantial and temporary as a mirage, bubbles in the water, or dream fantasies and figures.
If you live day by day with the unwavering adoration of the Buddha in your heart, it will one day blossom like a fragrant lotus flower soaring from the muck and mud.

The Essence
of the Korean Buddhist
Practices

03

Mantra Practice

What is the Power of Mantra?

Incantations, or mantras are sentences, words or syllables considered capable of spiritual transformation. Mantra or incantation is practiced to still and develop the mind by relying on the mystical power vested in the special words. The use of mantras can be found in the scriptural sources of all Buddhist schools, and its practice is universal throughout the regions of eastern religious traditions, not only in India and Southeast Asia but also in northern and far Eastern Asia.

Language is a tool to communicate agreed and shared meanings. However, mantra is believed to have an inherent meaning independent of the common understanding, manifestations of the ultimate reality. Due to their transcendental power, it has been reverently referred to with various names, such as mantra, dharani and paritta. They are also translated diversely into Chinese and called such as 'words of truth,' 'total retention,' 'words that guard,' 'divine words,' or 'words of knowledge.'

What mysterious power do mantras have? Mantras or dharanis protect the one who chants them from malign influences and calamities. With all the merits attained by the Buddhas and Bodhisattvas wholly packed into the short spell like speech, mantras not only help the faithful with mundane purposes such as attaining wealth and long life, but also grant the wisdom and capabilities equal to the Buddha. It has served a wide range of functions in religious rituals, from material gains to spiritual attainment.

Most of mantras are made of incomprehensible phonics. Why all these cryptic syllables? Language is an important vehicle that carries

human intents and understanding. But it is a limited vessel. It is virtually impossible to convey 100% of our thoughts or experiences to the other person. Likewise, the other person will never be able to get 100% of his thoughts or experiences across to us either. Frustration all too commonly ensues when the other person misunderstands or distorts our meaning despite the best efforts to be clear.

The Buddha's teachings are uncannily profound and frequently unfathomable. Of course he kindly spared no efforts to clarify the concepts and articulate them logically for the vast majority of people. But it is still not easy to perfectly grasp his experiences of enlightenment through the medium of words because they are simply outside the limits of our normal perceptive cognizance, which is too constrained to fully contain their wisdom. Language is also too flawed an instrument to perfectly accommodate the majestic teachings of the Buddha. As such, the Buddha used mantras, 'vocal sounds that come before language' to express what is essentially beyond the bounds of human cognition.

Fearlessly abandon the erroneous intermediary of words, which are solely based on our imperfect knowledge and understanding, and instead choose the 'words of truth' by the Buddha himself. Enlightened rapture will mystically spring forth from within our mind and body.

Doctrinal *Ground*

The *Heart Sutra*, the most venerated sutra among Korean Buddhists, says:

"Therefore know that Prajnaparamita is the great transcendent mantra, is the bright mantra, is the supreme mantra, which is able to relieve all suffering and is true, not false. So proclaim the mantra which says:

Gate gate paragate parasamgate bodhi svaha."

This last passage from the *Heart Sutra* demonstrates that mantra practice has been integral to the Mahayana system as a means to conquer calamities and attain the perfect enlightenment, or prajnaparamita. Nagarjuna explicated in his *Mahaprajnaparamita Sastra,*

"Of all mantras, prajnaparamita mantra is the most exulted one. It is because the Buddha always imparts the merits of the perfect wisdom to all sentient beings. Heretics use mantra for material gains, therefore it may arouse afflictions. And if acts malignant to other live beings accompany the practice, it can cause rebirth in the realms of hell, hungry ghosts or animals. Incantations by wicked heretics can go out of hand, recklessly following the dictate of fury, avarice and stupidity. On the other hand, the mantra of prajnaparamita melts away all obsessions, even the attachment to samadhi and nirvana. Maladies of anger and desire simply dissolve in the face of this mantra."

Mantra practice was cultivated into a more elaborate system, eventually developing into esoteric or tantric Buddhism. The well-known esoteric Buddhist scriptures are: the *Mahavairocana Sutra*, the *Vajrasekhara Sutra*, the *Karandavyuha*, and the *Putixinlun*.

Mahavairocana Buddha is the most venerated refuge in Esoteric Buddhism. An omnipotent being, he never appears or disappears and he is like the sun in the sky evaporating all distresses and delusions. In esoteric Buddhism, each and every one of the phenomena of the universe is recognized as the sacred manifestation of Mahavairocana himself. All the evil and the good, the ugly and the beautiful, the joyful and the tormented are all intrinsically not at all different from Mahavairocana Buddha himself.

If so, why are the Buddhas and Bodhisattvas happy, while the sentient beings are not? Esoteric practitioners would reply, "The only difference between you and the Buddha lies in the act of deed, speech and thought. If you start right away behaving, talking and thinking like them, you are as happy and astute as the Buddha, and all human anguishes are insignificant specks of cloud under the radiance of the sun."

Then, the question is what are the deeds, speech and thoughts of the Buddha? Let's listen to the esoteric practitioners a little more.

"If you find yourself wondering what the act of a Buddha is, just mirror three secret acts of the Buddha. Trace mudras with the hands in the air, the very secret hand gestures of the Buddha himself; intone mantra with the mouth, the very words of the Buddha, and; heed with your thought the secret samadhi of the Buddha. This is called the Three Secret Practices of Esotericism. If your acts coincide with those of the Buddha, you will be immediately visited upon by vast abilities and wisdom of Mahavairocana. Imagine you are in front of a vault filled with rare and precious treasures. But it is locked. The three secret acts are like keys to the lock. The instance those keys unfasten the door, you become tremendously wealthy and realize that the treasures have always belonged to you."

That is why esoteric Buddhists do not tell us to "be a Buddha." Instead, they urge us to "act like one right here and now."

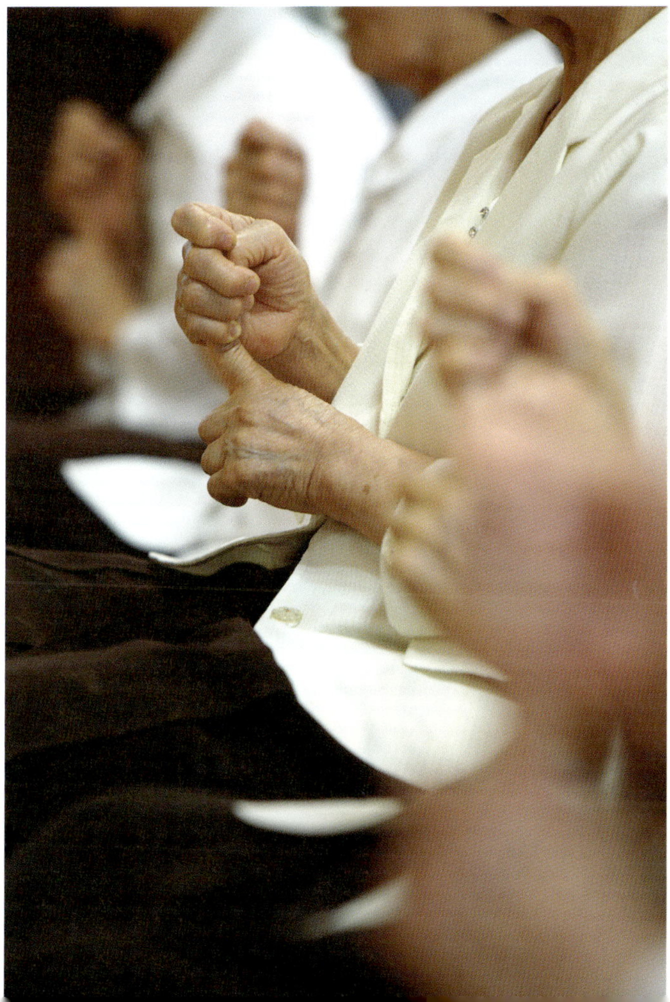

▪ Vajra mudra, Hongwon Simin-dang Temple

History of Mantra Practice in Korean Buddhism

A Japanese text called the *History of Zenkoji Temple* wrote, "The *Sutra of Seeking Avalokitesvara* transmitted from Baekje was distributed and garnered a large following." This sutra describes four kinds of Avalokitesvara dharanis and the merits one can earn by practicing them, quoting, "All negative karmas of the past lives disappear upon hearing the recitation of the name of Avalokitesvara and his dharanis." This shows that mantra practice was already flourishing in Korean Peninsula during the Three Kingdoms period.

The *Memorabilia of the Three Kingdoms* also recorded, "When the Tang Chinese army invaded Silla in 670, 12 monks led by Myeongnang officiated the secret ritual of *munduru* to summon the typhoon that defeated the invading troops." The *Sutra of Consecration* prescribes in detail the procedures for the secret ritual of *munduru*. According to the Sutra, *munduru* is produced by carving out the names of the god beings guarding the 5 directions of the north, south, west, east and the center. *Munduru* is believed to be accorded with magical endowments to ward off all disasters and attract only auspicious tidings.

Later in Silla, two esoteric Buddhist sects called Sinin Order and Chongji Order were founded. The dharani practice of these Orders was mostly focused on worldly benefits, such as defending the nation, forestalling calamities and extending lifespan.

Master Euisang (625~702) also implored in his written dedication of vows to Avalokitesvara "I hereby avow my dedication to lead all sentient beings to chant the *mahakarunikacitta* dharani (the Dharani of

Great Compassion) and the names of Bodhisattvas so that all beings would enter the samadhi of vast oceanic calm." The Dharani of Great Compassion is none other than the Thousands Hands dharani which is the locus of intense devotional practice in Korean Buddhism still today, attesting to the pervasiveness of this particular dharani even during the Three Kingdom Period.

During the Goryeo period, the *Suramgama Sutra* (*Heroic March Sutra*) became popular as Master Euicheon (1055~1101) brought from China related commentaries and Lee Jahyeon gave a series of lectures on the topic. The practice of reciting the *Suramgama* dharani (Heroic March dharani) found in the seventh fascicle of the Sutra also started in this period.

In the later Goryeo period, esoteric Buddhism was widely propagated due to the influences of the Yuan Dynasty where Tibetan Buddhism became prominent at the court. The famous six syllable mantra "Om mani padma hum" and related practice were received at this time. Six syllable mantra practices are conducted following the instructions in the Tibetan text *Manibkab Bbum*. Several edited or extracted versions of this text are circulated to this day in Korea, such as the *Yukja daemyeongwang gyeong*. Inscriptions of Om mani padma hum can be commonly seen carved onto the brahma bells or roof tiles of Korean temples today.

In modern Korea, Master Suwol (1855~1928) and Master Yongseong are well-known popularizers of the Thousands Hands dharani and the six syllable mantra.

▪ Mantra Practice, Baekryeon-am Hermitage

Mantra Practice *Today*

▪ Mantra Practice, Baekryeon-am Hermitage

The *Seokmun euibeom* is a comprehensive manual on the Buddhist rituals and ceremonies complied by An Jinho in 1935. Still considered a standard text for rituals by modern day Korean temples it lists 117 dharanis, including mantras for daily us. To most Korean Buddhists, the mantra is a familiar part of their religious life, but the practice is rarely an agent for significant spiritual experiences.

Currently, Jogye-sa Temple, Baekyang-sa Temple, Deokyang Seon Center, Gyongmyeong Seon Center, Hongbeop-sa Temple and Nungin Sunwon adopt the practice of the Thousands Hands dharani and host regular Dharma assemblies to practice the dharani with the congregation.

Heroic March dharani was rediscovered by the public when Master Seongcheol (1912~1993), one of the giants of modern Korean Buddhism, included the dharani in the daily practice routine of his Bongam-sa Society in 1947. Baekryeon-am Hermitage of Haein-sa Temple, Jeongan-sa Temple, Jeongrim-sa Temple and Beopseong-sa Temple offer regular programs to practice the Heroic March dharani. Baekryeon-am Hermitage in particular also runs a 4-day program four times a year centering around the practice of Vairocana Dharmakaya mantra "Om avira hum cam svaha."

Master Heuidang Son Sanggyu (1902~1963) is a single most important contributor in modern Korean Buddhism who promoted mantra as a serious spiritual practice. He exclaimed that the three Secret Practices of Esotericism, especially in the form of chanting of the six syllable mantra "Om mani padma hum," allow one to realize the inherent pure dharmakaya of Vairocana within oneself, and confirm the essential exigency to dedicate oneself to the happiness of all beings in this very life. Many Simin-dang Temples across Korea coordinate the Three Secret Practice Assemblies every week. Chongji-sa Temple, Milin-sa Temple, Gwanseong-sa Temple, Silji-sa Temple, Jeongsim-sa Temple and Byeokryong-sa Temple also offer their congregation assemblies to practice the six syllable mantra.

How to Practice Mantra?

Methodology

Mantra can be practiced at any place, but a temple or a Simin-dang Temple is still preferable.

In case of practicing the Thousands Hands dharani or the Heroic March dharani, following procedures are recommended:

- Sweep the place and be prudent about one's speech and conduct.
- Bow to the Buddhas and Bodhisattvas who strive to save all beings.
- Ardently aspire to have one's wish fulfilled.
- Offer contrition to all one's past misconducts and wish them to be eliminated.
- Recite the mantra for the period or times one has determined.
- Dedicate all merits gained through this practice to the benefit of all beings.

When practicing the six syllable mantra, please follow the steps described below.

- Clean up the place for practice.
- Sit in lotus or half lotus position and calm one's breath.
- Pay homage to the 37 Buddhas and Bodhisattvas of Vajra dhatu mandala.
- Aspire to attain dharmakaya through this practice.
- Perform Dharmakaya mudra or Vajra mudra.

- Recite the mantra for the period or times one has determined.
- Repent all the past conducts stained with greed, anger and ignorance.
- Resolve never to stop striving to bring happiness to all beings.

One may chant mantra only in the mind, or speaking quietly or out loudly, similar to *yeombul* practice.

Benefits

Many Mahayana texts varyingly document the merits to be gained by mantra practice. The more repeatedly mentioned benefits are:

- Adverse situations resolve themselves.
- Difficulties with people disappear.
- Diseases are cured.
- Fear vanishes.
- Concentration becomes stronger and brighter.
- Confidence increases.
- Conduct and speech become more polite and gentle.
- One is not bothered by prejudices and becomes kinder to everyone.
- One becomes more determined and courageous.
- Compassion toward suffering neighbors arises.
- Defilements lose their torment and are replaced by the wisdom of the Buddha.
- One realizes the inherent Buddhahood within oneself.

They are not just superstitious claims made by archaic texts. Many mantra practitioners still experience all these merits and benefits every day.

1 2
3 4

1. 2. Mantra Practice, Baekryeon-am Hermitage
3. 4. Mantra Practice, Hongwon Simin-dang Temple

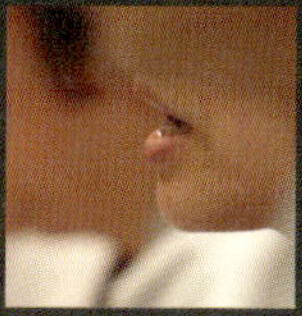

Musing From a Guide

If something nags and bothers you,
Sit quietly and recite mantras.
How mysterious:
Gone is the desire to grasp more, replaced by generosity to give.
Gone is the hatred, replaced by forgiveness.
Gone is the competitive need to beat others, replaced by the yearning to help them.
Gone is laziness, replaced by the eagerness to work harder.
Gone is the distraction and excitement, replaced by serenity.
Gone is the confusion and darkness, replaced by clarity and radiance.
How mysterious.
Now, just follow and act upon this mind.
Nothing matters to you anymore.

The Essence
of the Korean Buddhist
Practices

04

Sutra Reading Practice

What is Sutra Reading Practice?

The first thing we do when we venture into a new land is to consult a map. Likewise, when we decide to travel through the realm of the Buddha, we need to learn his teachings first, and his teachings are contained in the sutras. The purpose of reading sutras is to familiarize oneself with the Buddha's teachings. The act of "reading a sutra" can take diverse forms; we can follow the lines with eyes, read out loud, chant or sing and dance along with a tune or movement. The word 'read' in Korean can have alternate meanings, such as 'learn,' 'understand' or 'transmit,' depending on the context. Therefore, sutra reading encompasses a whole range of practice activities involving the hearing, understanding, memorizing, explaining, singing, narrating and propagating of the Buddhist philosophy.

Even during his lifetime, learning his philosophical views was considered a priority in joining the Buddha's path. The *Dhammapada*, short, versified phrases of the Buddha's teachings, the scriptures with commentaries and the vinaya, the precepts for the Buddhist monastic community were read and recited extensively from the very inception of the Buddhist tradition.

In the long history of Buddhism, sutra reading has been delivered in association and accompaniment with many purposes and events. It has been performed to understand and preserve the Buddhist doctrines; to embody and attain the tranquility of nirvana and the wisdom of perfect enlightenment; to validate one's experiences during the practice against the authentic teachings; to propagate; to offer gratitude to those who make generous donations; to exalt the Buddha's wisdom and merits; to ward off calamities and cumulate good fortune; heal illnesses; to pray for the souls of the dearly departed, and last but not least; to secure the peace and stability of the regime.

The Buddha devoted his life for our happiness. He showed us what the pain we suffer is made of, why it feels so horrible, and then he tried to teach us what to do to make it all go away. But the understanding does not make it perish instantaneously. Nor are we immune to the bouts of recurrences. Why is that so? We are disastrously good at harrying ourselves into tight spots. At the slightest drop of our attention, all the old corrupting habits in thoughts, speech and deeds sneak back right on us. In order to unlearn them, we need to gather and awaken ourselves to new ways of life, patiently and repetitively, almost for as long as it took for these bad habits to be firmly established and deeply rooted in the first place. The words of the Buddha are the essential element in this process.

The Buddha's teachings are mirrors. They reflect who we are here in this very moment, not the projections of our memories or imagination. The mirror unerringly tells us the reality of what are we thinking, saying and doing exactly as it is.

Suppose we see a person ridiculously wandering around the street with ketchup smeared all over his mouth. We can be fairly certain that the person never looked into a mirror before he left his home. Most of us commit wrongful acts because we are unaware of what exactly we are doing. It is indeed rare someone goes out of his way to destroy himself and others when the suffering it causes is clearly understood. The Buddha puts a mirror in front of us so that we can see ourselves that our current action would lead to misery or joy. Consulting the mirror stops us in our track and steers us toward the right direction. Sutra reading practice entails hearing, learning, memorizing and reciting the Buddha's teachings so that our life will stay on the right course. Inscribe his words into the heart day by day, just as we take shower and look into the mirror every morning. It will transform us into a composed, caring and sagacious person.

Doctrinal *Ground*

The *Samyuttanikaya* records, "Anuruddha, one of the principle disciples of the Buddha, was staying at Jetavana Monastery in Savatthi. He woke up at dawn and recited sutra from his memory." The Chinese translation of the *Samyuktagama also* says, "There was a merchant named Upasaka. He woke up early at dawn, sat quietly, stilled and focused his mind, and chanted loudly gathas from the *Dhammapada* and other sutras and the conditions for paramita."

These texts indicate that the Buddhists from the very beginning of the tradition started their day by reciting the Buddha's words. The *Sutra of Vipasyin Buddha*, compiled from the excerpts of the early Pali canon the *Dirghagama* quotes, "If one learns and memorizes sutras with joy, and mulls over and recites them whether going or coming, standing or sitting, walking or lying down, all delusions will perish and the samsaric cycle will cease turning. Suffering will end and only comforts and happiness will remain." The *Ekottarikagama* also counts 'keeping mind wholly encapsulated in the Buddha's teachings by reciting them' as one of the five ways to eradicate defilements, presenting yet another proof that sutra reading was one of the primary practices from the dawn of the Buddhist tradition.

Sutra reading was raised to an even loftier place in the Mahayana era. The *Heart Sutra* exclaims "If one wholeheartedly and diligently hears, learns, recites, ponders over, explains, copies and distributes this profound truth of prajnaparamita, the person will achieve in this lifetime the states of stream-enterer (srota-apanna), once-returner (sakrdagamin), non-returner (an-agamin) and the foe-destroyer (arhat)." The *Diamond Sutra* wrote, "Let me ask you Subhuti. If a person filled over ten thousand galaxies with the seven treasures for the purpose of compassion, charity, and giving alms, would this person not gain great merit and spread much happiness? Then suppose another person understood only four lines of this Sutra, but nevertheless took it upon themselves to explain these lines to someone else. This person's merit would be even greater than the other person's." The Mahayana tradition obviously viewed the reading of sutras as the most direct way to achieve Buddhist sainthood, and the offering of teachings as the finest form of generosity.

The *Parinirvana Sutra* goes even further, saying, "If one soaks the skins of a big drum in poison and strikes it in the middle of a crowd, whether they intend it or not, those who hear them will all die. This sutra is the same. The sound of this sutra being recited will expel all greed, anger and ignorance from those who hear it, wherever they are and whatever they do." Even passively hearing somebody else chanting the sutra, one can progress forward on the path of practice.

History of Sutra Reading Practice in Korean Buddhism

There is no Buddhism without the Buddha's teachings. Therefore, the 1,700 years of history of Korean Buddhism is indeed the history of Koreans learning and transmitting the Buddha's words. Buddhism was first introduced to Korea in 372, the 2nd year of Goguryeo's King Sosurim. According to the *Annals of the Three Kingdoms*, Chinese monk Sundo was sent by Fu Jian (337~385) of Former Qin, bringing texts and statues with him. As Buddhism became the state religion, sutra reciting was added to the private and public ceremonies solemnized to pray for wellbeing and prosperity. The *Annals of the Goryeo Dynasty* recorded numerous occasions where esteemed masters were invited to recite and lecture on the sutra and pray for the stability and prosperity of the state and the royal court. The *Annals of the Joseon Dynasty* also cited an event where "in his 5th year (1459), King Sejo celebrated a sutra reading assembly at the Royal Buddha Hall in Gyeongbok Palace on the Buddha's birthday," confirming sutra reading as a ritual continued during the Joseon Dynasty despite the national policy of suppressing Buddhism and promoting Neo-Confucianism.

When sutra reading was performed for ritualistic purposes, the intonation was made into a hymn like tune, accompanied by musical instruments such as bells, wooden hand-bells and drums in order to facilitate the ease of understanding and the congregational chanting. This has developed into an art form called *beompae*. The *Annuls of the Three Kingdoms* observed a performance of *beompaes* early as in the 7th century and according to *Jingamguksa daegongtapbi* (*Inscriptions on the Tombstone of the National Preceptor Jingam*) it became widely held in the early 9th century throughout the Peninsula. Traditional *beompae* ceremonies are being played in many Korean temples still to this day.

Sutra Reading Practice *Today*

▪ Sutra Reading Practice, Traditional Buddhism Cultural Center

Virtually all Buddhist temples, centers and organizations in Korea offer one program or another that reads, recites and lectures on sutras. Sutra reading is the single most important daily curriculum at Dharma seminaries, the traditional centers for educating monastics, and it is also the integral part of morning and evening services with a ceremony at 11am to offer a meal to the Buddha at the Buddhist temple. Chanting sutras with the congregation followed by commentaries is a standard feature of any Buddhist assembly. Sutra reading often goes together with visiting Buddhist friends in the hospital or Buddhist funeral service. Buddhist colleges scattered throughout the country all run sutra reading and learning programs, and there are many lay societies and clubs whose members are pledged to daily sutra reading practice. The Diamond Sutra Reading Society, the True Dharma Study Institute and Bogwang Seon Center are particularly famous for their systematic approach in teaching sutra reading practice.

The most commonly recited sutras by Korean Buddhist are: the *Heart Sutra*, the *Thousand Hands Sutra*, the *Diamond Sutra*, the *Flower Garland Sutra*, the *Lotus Sutra*, the *Amitabha Sutra*, the *Perfect Enlightenment Sutra* and the *Heroic March Sutra*.

In addition, the texts by eminent teachers were often equated to and as cherished as those by the Buddha himself, such as Master Wonhyo's *Balsim suhaengjang* (meaning "Awaken Your Mind to Practice"), and Master Euisang's the *Song of Dharma Nature*. Koreans also adore discourse records by Patriarchs, such as the *Platform Sutra*, the *Xinxinming*, the *Song of Enlightenment*, and the *Song of Impermanence*.

How to Practice Sutra Reading?

Methodology

Sutra reading in a broader sense includes hearing, understanding, memorizing, explicating, chanting, singing and disseminating. Let's focus on the chanting aspect of sutra reading, which is most relevant to the deepening of an individual practitioner's spiritual experiences.

When chanting a sutra, one can choose to recite the whole text, just core phrases or gathas (verses) or the title. One also can stand up, kneel down, or sit in lotus position or on the chair.

Please bear the following preliminaries in mind before starting sutra reciting practice.

- Understand the text to be recited sufficiently.
- Do it regularly at a set time and place.
- Be discreet with your mind as well as your conduct.
- Imagine the Buddha is sitting right in front of you.
- Keep the spine straight.
- Reciting for too long a time may unnecessarily strain the body.

Below are the steps recommended to be followed:

- Clean the place of practice.
- Take refuge in the Buddha, Dharma and Sangha.
- Vow to attain enlightenment through the words of the Buddha.
- Chant the sutra-opening mantra "Om aranam arada" three times.
- Recite the title of the sutra three times.
- Recite the sutra for the period or the amount of time one has determined.
- Vow to put into action the understanding that comes as the result of sutra reading.

▪ Sutra Reading Practice, Unmun-sa Temple

Benefits

The benefits of sutra reading practice were compiled into several books dedicated to recording the miracles of the Buddha's blessings. Some of the more notable ones are:

- The Buddhas and Bodhisattvas and heavenly beings appear and avail protection.
- One is saved from the imminent threat of death.
- Diseases are cured and health is restored.
- Negative karmas perish.
- Words and deeds become gentler.
- A firm faith in the Buddha's teachings takes shape.
- When faced with a difficulty, the most relevant solution among the teachings of the Buddha is recalled automatically.
- One quickly notices when anger and greed arise.
- Suffering vanishes, replaced by the well spring of the Buddha's wisdom.
- One's daily routine naturally follows the footsteps of the Buddha.
- One gains rebirth in the Buddha Land.
- *Sarira* is found in the ashes after cremation.

They are not just happenings in the past. They still occur to numerous sutra reading practitioners here and now.

Musing From a Guide

Wake up at an early dawn
To open the day with the words of the Buddha.
If chanting aloud is too much, hear others read.
If the whole book is too overwhelming, read just a phrase.
That phrase will be a mirror that reflects
Your distracted actions, coarse speech and runaway thoughts
That hold you in their thrall.
You are helpless when you do not know;
When you do know, you are not powerless anymore.
Keep looking into the mirror.
Someday, calm poise, soft words and tranquil mind
Become you.
Day by day in front of the mirror,
May your transformation be welcomed by everybody,
Especially by yourself.
Then, make the gift of the mirror to your friends.
May they be as happy as I am.

The Essence
of the Korean Buddhist
Practices

05

Sutra Copying Practice

What is Sutra Copying?

▪ Stupa enshrining the *sarira* of Sakyamuni Buddha, Beopju-sa Temple

Sutra copying is the practice of writing down the content of the sutra by hand. The sutras are the records of the oral teachings of the Buddha himself, but when a broader definition of 'the teachings of the Buddha' is to apply, the regulatory framework for the monastic community (vinaya), scholastic reworkings of doctrinal material appearing in the sutras (abhidharma), philosophical treatises and exegeses, and the words of Seon patriarchs can all be considered suitable objects for sutra copying practice. One can copy the whole volume of a canonical text or critical passages from them, or only repeat the titles of the texts. In a sense, writing down a single character of 'the Buddha' can constitute sutra copying practice.

Writing is considered a superior means of transferring knowledge and information than oral transmission. It is far more accurate and less prone to accidental distortions and unintended changes. Writing, therefore, has long been a preferred vehicle for the dissemination of the Buddha's teachings. India and other Southeast Asian countries used material made out of the bark of palm trees called pattra to write scriptures on, while in Northeast Asia, paper was available from earlier on. The Buddha's words were also inscribed on the surface of rocks or trees, which later led to the development of printing.

Scriptural texts have long been treasured as the object of veneration as well as tools for learning. After the Buddha entered parinirvana, his followers erected stupas all over the Indian subcontinent to enshrine his relics, hair, effects and ashes from the cremation, and these stupas formed an extensive network of pilgrimage sites. In the Mahayana era, scriptures were deemed as part of the sacred relics of the Buddha, or *sarira*, qualified to be enshrined in pagodas or stupas and worshipped. To Mahayana Buddhists, copying sutras is a particularly pious act of spiritual regeneration that breathes new life into *sarira* and the Buddha's words.

Copying the Buddha's words by hand has been a practice of many fold purposes. It was carried out to disseminate the teachings of the Buddha; learn and understand his words; exalt his benevolence and blessings; invoke divine intervention for the protection of the state; cure illnesses; repent past transgressions; achieve longevity, or; commend the souls of the dead to the Buddhas and Bodhisattvas. A common thread running through all these is the intent to embody and manifest the understanding of the Buddha's teachings.

▪ Stupa enshrining the *sarira* of Sakyamuni Buddha, Bongjeong-am Hermitage

라가지마세요

Doctrinal Ground

The *Sutra on the Dharani of the Pure Immaculate Light* commands, "The dharani be copied and a stupa be erected along major roads to enshrine the copy. Many sentient creatures will pass by the stupa, be they birds, four legged beasts, butterflies, spiders or ants, and they will all be delivered from the realms of hell and reborn in heavens." The *Diamond Sutra* also exclaimed, "Wherever this *Sutra* shall be, it will become a sacred ground to which countless gods and asuras will bring offerings. Such a place is a shrine and should be venerated with magnificent ceremonies, and offerings of flowers and incense."

Mahayana Buddhist revered the act of copying sutras, and the pilgrims worshipped copied manuscripts sealed inside pagodas with the offering of flowers and incense. It is considered a viable way to practice the Bodhisattva act of liberating all beings from the sufferings of defilements through the teachings of the Buddha. In the Mahayana tradition, sutra copying is one of more potent practices that merit Buddhahood or rebirth in one of the Buddha realms. The *Flower Garland Sutra* says:

"Do not rouse suspicions upon hearing this wish. Receive, read, memorize, write down and teach others what you learn as best as you can. Those who do this shall have all their wishes fulfilled just by mere thoughts and they will earn inconceivable and incalculable blessings. Such persons will save all beings from misery, transcend life and death and finally be reborn in the Paradise of Amitabha Buddha."

The *Sutra of Attaining Longevity and Eliminating All Crimes* says, "If one receives, carries, write down and recite this Sutra with utmost devotion, one will attain the indestructible body of the Buddha… or have his life span extended. Even if one contracts a disease and dies, the death will be pain free." The *Sutra of Cause and Effect in Three Ages* asserts "If one writes down this sutra and spreads the copies far and wide, his future descendents will enjoy abundant prosperity and have a bright future." This textual evidence indicates sutra copying practice was considered an effective means to attract worldly favors.

Further, the *Flower Garland Sutra* has a passage describing how practitioners "peel the stripes of skin off of their own bodies and use them as paper, split bones to make brushes, and siphon off the blood to use it as ink and write down a mound of sutras as big as Mt. Sumeru," indicating how sacred the act of sutra copying was to the Mahayana tradition.

History of Sutra Copying Practice in Korean Buddhism

Currently, the oldest example of sutra copying still extant in Korea is the *Sutra on the Dharani of the Pure Immaculate Light* which was discovered within a reliquary inside a five-story stone pagoda in Nawon-ri, Gyeongju. But the exact date is unknown.

The oldest manuscript of sutra copying with a known date is the 'Two Silla Period Scrolls of the *Flower Garland Sutra* written on paper' produced between 754 and 755, designated as the National Treasure No. 196. This copy had been enshrined within the five-story stone pagoda at Hwaeom-sa Temple. On the cover of this manuscript is the elaborate frontispiece depicting the images of the Buddhas and Bodhisattvas painted in gold and silver powder, and the roller is decorated with crystals, which are set with *sarira*. The *History of Jikji-sa Temple* recorded, "In the late Silla period, King Gyeongsun had a copy of the Heart Sutra made in gold ink, and the king himself wrote the title of the sutra." During the Silla period, sutra copying was clearly regarded as an act of spiritual devotion warranting the use of gold powder, and thus produced manuscripts were sealed inside the pagoda and venerated widely.

The tradition of sutra copying flourished during the Goryeo Dynasty. According to the *Annals of the Goryeo Dynasty*, several copies of the *Flower Garland Sutra* and the *Lotus Sutra* were produced in gold and silver letters. King Myeongjong went so far as to establish the Sutra Copying Bureau in 1181 to train specialized scribes. The copies produced by the Bureau became renowned for its beauty and precision, so the Goryeo's monk scribes were internationally in high demand and were sent to China several times at the request of the Yuan court. Goryeo people's zeal to duplicate the teachings of the Buddha on paper and make them proliferate resulted in the monumental project of carving the printing woodblocks for the entire set of canonical scriptures. However, the original set of woodblocks were destroyed by fire during the Mongol invasion in 1232 and King Gojong ordered the re-creation of the Tripitaka Koreana, which took 16 years from 1236 to 1251 and is currently stored at Haein-sa Temple.

With the advent of woodblock printing technology, which made the mass distribution of Buddhist texts possible, the tradition of hand-copying sutras began to die out, and all but disappeared with the suppression of Buddhism in the Joseon Dynasty. Sutra copying only for its devotional aspect falteringly continued into Joseon with copies still remaining, but they hardly displayed a comparable artistic effect. Notable in the Joseon period is sutra copying using human blood, compensating for the lack of royal or aristocratic patronage with ardor. Seon Master Yeonggi's copy of the *Amitabha Sutra*, which he wrote in his own blood in the winter of 1852 at Jijang-am Hermitage in Mt. Bogae in Cheolwon, is extant today.

▪ Haein-sa Temple Janggyeong Panjeon, the Depositories for the Tripitaka Koreana Woodblocks (UNESCO World Heritage)

Sutra Copying Practice *Today*

▪ Sutra Copying Practice, Myogak-sa Temple

A vast majority of Buddhist texts available in Korea these days are printed editions. However, devotional sutra copying is still practiced today, in the form of copying short sutras or passages. Mangong, Gyeongbong, Hyobong, Choengdam and Seoong are some of the eminent Seon masters of modern Korea who variably copied the Heart Sutra, gathas, and Patriarchs' words and handed them out. Buddhist monks today produce a large quantity of calligraphed copies of the letter '佛' (the Buddha) or phrases such as '眞空妙有 (the true emptiness is marvelous existence)' or '一切唯心造 (all things are created by the mind alone)' and regularly give them out as gifts to their congregation.

Sutra copying is carried out as a Buddhist practice at; Myogak-sa Temple, Guryeong-sa Temple, Bulhyangji, Geukrak-sa Temple, Eunhae-sa Temple, Beophwajeong-sa Temple, Nungin Sunwon and Hongbeop-sa Temple. Myogak-sa Temple in particular generates enthusiastic responses by first teaching about the sutra to be copied, thus helping the practitioner clearly understand the meaning of the practice and the blessings earned by it. Sutra copying practice at Myogak-sa Temple is now famous among foreigners, widely attracting seekers of spirituality from all over the world. The Korea Sutra Copying Research Institute also offers a systematic program on the traditional sutra copying practice.

Sutras most favored by Koreans for hand copying practice are the *Flower Garland Sutra*, the *Lotus Sutra*, the *Diamond Sutra* and the *Heart Sutra*.

How to Practice Sutra Copying?

Methodology

Traditionally, copying sutras has been considered as reverent an act as dedicating *sarira* to a pagoda. Therefore, the ancient sutra copying practitioners proceeded with utmost deference. The records on the making of Silla period scrolls of the *Flower Garland Sutra* wrote:

> "The mulberry trees, whose barks are used to make papers, were irrigated with perfumed water. After the trees were grown, everyone involved in sutra copying, from the workers who strip the bark from the trees, craftsmen who produce papers, calligraphers, artisans who paint frontispieces and *parinama* (Buddhist images) to common errand boys were all required to take the Bodhisattva vow and put on a special dietary regime. If a participant in the process urinated or defecated, lied down to sleep or ate, he was admitted back to the workshop only after taking a bath in perfumed water."

▪ Sutra Copying Practice, Myogak-sa Temple

It would not be feasible to follow all the steps ancient Buddhists honored, but their devotion should not be forgotten. When one engages in sutra copying one should:

- Understand the content of the sutra sufficiently.
- Preferably practice at a regular time and place.
- Take a bath and put on clean clothes.
- Straighten one's back while writing.
- Not store the completed copies in a dirty place.
- When making a gift of copied sutra, make sure the receiver would treasure it as much as the practitioner does.

When practicing sutra copying, please follow the steps below:

- Sweep the place clean.
- Prepare clean paper and pens.
- Take refuge in the Buddha, Dharma and Sangha
- Confess to the Buddha one's most ardent wish.
- Recite the passage before writing.
- Calm the breath and still the mind.
- Copy the sutra as much as one has decided.
- Read aloud the part that one just copied.
- Dedicate all the merits earned by the practice to your neighbors.

Benefits

Many cases are cited in various *Miracle Stories* as well as in scriptures and commentaries on how the practitioners of sutra copying were blessed with benevolent results, such as:

- Many Buddhas and Bodhisattvas appear as guardians.
- Calamities such as wars and famines disappear.
- Diseases are cured and health is restored.
- Negative karmas perish and one earns worldly gains such as wealth and fame.
- One always does one's best and stays calm all the time.
- Body smells fragrant.
- Suffering vanishes, replaced by the state of samadhi.
- A firm faith in the Buddha's teachings takes place both in body and mind.
- One gains rebirth in the Buddha realm.
- *Sarira* is found in the ashes after cremation.

One cannot copy the whole sutra in one go. Each letter has to be calligraphed carefully. Our writing reflects it the moment the thought gets astray, as the stroke becomes askew. Therefore, sutra copying is a good exercise to learn how to contain distracted and scattered thoughts and strengthen the focus of mind, as much as a religious practice.

Musing From a Guide

Unfurl the snow white paper,
Dip the brush in the pitch black ink and
Write down the words of truth
Resonating through your heart.
First, cultivate yourself
Sound of body and serene of mind.
Then really understand the teaching
And write them down
Until they are carved onto the bone and seeped into the marrow.
Write them letter by letter,
Like laying one brick at a time to build
A magnificent pagoda dedicated to the Buddha's *sarira*.
Then, make a gift of the pagoda of *sarira*, of dharmakaya
To the neighbors living in pain and misery.
Like a pagoda that grants wishes to all those who pray to it,
Your writing of beauty and truth
Will bring abounding blessings to you and your neighbors.
Write down the words of the Buddha, sincere of heart.
Page after page,
One neighbor after another is brought into bliss and serenity.

The Essence
of the Korean Buddhist
Practices

06

Bowing Practice

What is Bowing?

Bowing is a physical way of expressing respect to others in Asia. There are three kinds of bowing in Buddhism: one can stand up with palms together and the head dipped low, kneel with palms together, or bow with both knees, both elbows and the head hitting the ground ("five-point veneration"). The last position, throwing the whole body to the ground in prostration with our heads lower than others' feet, is considered the most respectful form of bowing practice.

The highest point of the body is the forehead, the lowest is the feet. Placing my loftiest point lower than the other person's bottommost is showing total respect and unmitigated humility. Koreans bow to everyone: the Buddha, Bodhisattvas, parents, teachers, seniors, spouses, friends, relatives, religious figures and strangers. Korean Buddhists find it an important spiritual practice to humble themselves even to those who are junior in age and social position, inferior in intelligence and competence and those who are critical, abusive, angry and chiding.

Why do we practice something that is seemingly demeaning? In short, we do it to be happy. The Buddha taught us that the root cause of the fundamental human condition of unsatisfactoriness lies in the clinging to the non-existent "I." This foolishness leads people to create the illusionary dichotomy of "I" and "others" and we plunge ourselves into competition, striving to outdo others. This is called arrogance.

This bad habit puts us at the mercy of rollercoaster moods, making us puffed up with pride, dejected, joyful and sad in turn. If we can always beat challengers and stay on top, we may be able to fend off this sense of primordial unhappiness, perpetually creeping up on us. But deep down we all know that it just cannot be so. We will eventually be foiled and depressed at the sight of ourselves on the losing side. Arrogance can never lead us to true happiness. Bowing is the best cure for such conceit. Changes of mind can come to fruition before those of the body, but sometimes the body takes the lead in the process of the transformation of mind. If we are acting proudly, we are ignorant of the truth of non-self.

Bow to the person in front of us right now. Dip the head to the lowest point. We will come face to face with ourselves trapped in the concept of illusionary "I," acting conceited, sprouting nonsense, blustering and swaggering. If we cultivate humility with our body, the understanding of non-self will naturally grow in our mind. Such an understanding will transform a selfish and impetuous character ensnared in a desire to win into a kind and gentle person.

If someone upsets or distresses us, bow to the person with our head at his feet. Anger and grief cannot be resolved by violence. Violence only begets more violence. Revenge only prolongs the purgatorial time spent stewing in anxiety and hatred. Bow to those who are hostile to us, those who hurt us. Then, we will abide in true joy and peace.

Doctrinal Ground

Bowing can be dedicated to the Buddhas, Bodhisattvas, arhats, god beings, teachers, and even to parents. However, the Buddhas and Bodhisattvas are mostly commonly adored through prostration because respect and humility are aroused quickly. We can be easily moved by and supplicate without resistance to the Buddha, who is a fully enlightened being with perfect wisdom and boundless compassion, and Bodhisattvas, who attained incalculable merits through endless practice of the six paramitas. So many choose images of the Buddhas or Bodhisattvas, or pagodas where their *sarira* is enshrined as the objects of adoring reverence.

Nagarjuna wrote in his *Dasabhumika-vibhasa*, "Seekers of enlightenment, humbly supplicate to all the Buddhas of the universe, day and night, 24 hours a day, for repentance and for teachings. Rejoice in his teachings and share the delight with your neighbors. You will never fall off of the path toward perfect happiness." In the *Fayuanzhulin*, The Tang Dynasty monk Daoshi interpreted the above passage as:

"Many people are misled by delusions to believe in the dichotomy of 'I' and 'you,' and are drawn into the river of arrogance. As they are washed away towards the sea of suffering, even the thought of getting out of the river eludes them. Sages of all ages have taken pity on them and suggested this practice of worship and repentance. This is the practice of the highest potency, which will quickly lead to 'the state of non-retrogression' (avinivartaniya)."

The chapter on the Bodhisattva named Sadaparibhuta in the *Lotus Sutra* carries the story below, which also confirms the efficacy of bowing practice.

Once upon a time, there lived a monk who bowed to everyone he met, be they monks, nuns, laymen, or lay women, saying, "I respect you. I dare not despise you, because you are a precious being who will surely be a Buddha in the future." Because of his bowing, he was called Sadaparibhuta ("Bodhisattva that never despises"). He traveled far and wide, and whenever he caught sight of a person, he ran to them, bowed and hailed, "I respect you. I dare not despise you, because you will surely be a Buddha in the future." However, instead of thanking him, people heaped contempt on him, chasing him away by throwing rocks or wielding clubs, saying "You fool, who do you think you are, telling me what to be, be it a Buddha or not?" But the monk never got angry, humbly bowed and said, "I respect you. I dare not despise you, because you will surely be a Buddha in the future." A long time passed and Sadaparibhuta reincarnated in Kapilavatthu, a country established by Sakya clan, born of Suddhodana and Maya. He eventually attained perfect enlightenment and became none other than Sakyamuni, the historical Buddha.

History of Bowing Practice in Korean Buddhism

Since the introduction of Buddhism to the Korean Peninsula in the Three Kingdoms period, cases where supplication and penitence were used as the Buddhist practice are too numerous to specify. However, one of the best illustration can be found in the example of the Goryeo period monk Yose (1163~1245). His life story is described in the inscription on his tombstone at Baekryon-sa Temple in Mt. Manduk.

"He burst into laughter while lecturing on the *Contemplation Sutra*, when he came to a passage, 'This mind becomes the Buddha. This very mind is the Buddha.' Since then, his favorite topic became the *Contemplation Sutra*, on which he lectured with unhindered erudition and foresight. He recommended to his congregation the devotional practice of penitence and veneration, which he himself performed 12 times a day by paying homage to 53 Buddhas. He never slacked off on his commitment, never missing a day, whether in sweltering heat or freezing cold. His fellow monks called him 'Repenting Monk Seo'."

Given the fact that the *Jabi Doryang Chamboep*, which advocates the confession and contrition of one's past misconduct as an important practice, was hugely popular in the Goryeo and Joseon periods, bowing practice must have long been eagerly embraced by the masses of Korea.

Master Seongcheol (1912~1993), widely admired as the most esteemed Seon Master of our time in Korea, is well known for the emphasis he placed on bowing practice. Anyone seeking audience with him was required to dedicate 3,000 prostrations to the Buddha first. When asked about the reason for this rather stringent condition, he answered:

"What benefit seeing my face can possibly bring? That is why I use this opportunity to recommend bowing practice to people. When one supplicates to the noble Buddha, pride will subside and realization that all the hardships and distresses one suffers in life are in fact caused by none other than oneself would easily come. I also tell them to bow not for one's own happiness but for others. If one genuinely and sincerely forgives, understands, respects and loves others, one will experience unequalled peace and happiness. Such a person will naturally put others before him or herself and live for the happiness of others. Such a person will be welcomed and respected wherever he or she goes. What better benefit one can possibly think of?"

▪ Bowing Practice, Baekryeon-am Hermitage

Bowing Practice
Today

Buddhists prostrating in front of the statue of the Buddha can be easily observed in any temple in Korea. Bowing is perhaps the single most common Buddhist practice to Koreans. According to the 2003 survey by the Propagation Bureau of the Jogye Order, 32.3% of Buddhists polled engaged in contrition practice, by which they confess their past wrongful acts while prostrating.

Disciples of Master Seongcheol regularly host communal 3,000-bow practice programs at Jeongan-sa Temple, Jeongin-sa Temple, Jeongsim-sa Temple, Jeongrim-sa Temple, Gosimjeong-sa Temple, Haewoljeong-sa Temple, Gilsang Seon Center and Jeongsu-sa Temple. Baekryeon-am Hermitage in particular, where Master Seongcheol presided, dedicates 3,000 bows during the overnight practice every Friday.

Venerable Cheonggyeon modernized the bowing practice by analyzing the breathing and movement patterns involved with prostration and offering detailed instructions. He proved that bowing is a superb exercise designed to restore bodily health as well as cultivating the mind, popularizing it among non-Buddhists as well. He offers various bowing related programs and communal 3,000-bow practices once a month at his temple Beopwangjeong-sa as well as at Gunja Dharma Chapel, Geumjeong Dharma Chapel, Sincheon Dharma Chapel and Sangmu Dharma Chapel.

Hwagye-sa Temple, Gilsang-sa Temple, Bota-sa Temple and Jeonggak-won also organize the communal 3,000-bow practice every month. It is slightly different for each temple, depending on whether the bowing is accompanied by Buddha-recitation or contrition practice. Songgwang-sa Temple in Wanju also has a communal 3,000-bow practice on every 14th of the lunar calendar, and Geumgang Jeongto-sa Temple dedicates 1,000 prostrations to the Buddha every dawn. Nungin Sunwon, Bongeun-sa Temple and Gamlo-sa Temple also practice 3,000 bows 1~2 times a year

1 2
3

1. Bongeun-sa Temple
2. Songgwang-sa Temple in Wanju
3. Gilsang-sa Temple

One bow at every three steps

Bowing is more than a spiritual practice; it is a means to participate in society. Environmental activists have organized One Bow at Every Three Steps marches in protest against governmental policies such as Saemangeum development project and four river restoration project. Their essentially non-violent, peaceful rally has caused calm but resonating repercussions across society.

Bowing coupled with donation

Some temples such as Gilsang-sa Temple encourage their congregation to donate to charity the amount proportionate to the number of times one prostrates. This is well received as a way to put into practice the Mahayana Buddhist ideal of seeking the path to the enlightenment for the benefit of all beings.

How to Practice Bowing?

Methodology

Buddhists typically prostrate three times, 108 times, 1,080 times or 3,000 times. The simplest form of bowing practice is prostrating three times to show reverence to the Triple Gem of the Buddha, his teachings and the spiritual community. 108 bows represent 108 defilements, constituting a symbolic vow to overcome all afflictions.

We can bow any time, any place. But the presence of the Buddha or Bodhisattvas statues is preferable, even if it is not a temple. It is also better to do it every day, and at approximately the same time.

It is recommended to proceed according to the steps suggested below:

- Tidy up the surrounding area and light incense.
- Pay homage to the Triple Gem of the Buddha, Dharma and Sangha.
- Rouse the ardent aspiration to purify all defilements.
- Prostrate accordingly, 108, 1,080 or 3,000 times.
- Dedicate the merit accumulated by this practice to all your neighbors.

Bowing is carried out in one fluid motion. But it can be roughly broken down into: brining the palms together, kneeling down, lowering the body to the ground, kneeling back up and standing up for the ease of illustration.

- **Bring the palms together**: stand up with the feet touching each other and bring the palms together in front of the chest.
- **Kneel down**: kneel down with the spine straightened.
- **Lower the body to the ground**: extend the arms to touch the ground and lower your body to the ground until the forehead is between the hands. Spread the heels apart about 10cm, so that your buttocks rest between them. If all the limbs are touching the ground, flip and lift the palms up to the ears. This gesture symbolizes the uplifting of the Buddha's feet.
- **Kneel back up**: flip the palms back down to the ground, put your weight on your arms and push the body back into the kneeling position. Keep the spine straight and bring the heels back together.
- **Stand up**: stand up with the back straight.

Benefits

The *Eopbochabyeolgyeong* ("the *Sutra of Karmic Discrimination*") lists 10 merits achieved through the veneration of the Buddha.

- A sound and beautiful body is granted.
- Your words gain everyone's trust.
- Fear holds no sway.
- Both god beings and humans avail protection.
- Natural dignity is developed.
- Followers and admirers increase.
- Audiences with the Buddhas, Bodhisattvas and sages take place.
- Wealth, fame and life span grow.
- One gains rebirth in Buddha realms.
- Purification of defilements accelerates.

The benefits of bowing practice are very real in the present day, not just some mythic tales from archaic scriptural texts. There are numerous proven cases of various dire adversities overcome, terminal illnesses cured, and spiritual and mental health restored through bowing practice. Ms. Han Gyeong-hye for instance was diagnosed with cerebral palsy and almost died at the age of 7, but was able to defeat the disability through three occasions of 10,000-bow practices and grew up to be a fine artist.

Bowing practice develops a humble mind. It also disentangles the complicated web of thoughts and focuses the mind into the crystal clear state of samadhi. Once a practitioner stays with that serene stillness, wisdom to see the reality as it is emerges. Even as a purely non-religious exercise, bowing cultivates patience, heightens concentration, boosts blood circulation and enhances muscle strength. Bowing especially helps when one's heart is heavy with worries about the uncertain future, or the head is cluttered with conflicting thoughts upon the prospect of having to make an important decision.

▪ Bowing Practice, Tongdo-sa Temple

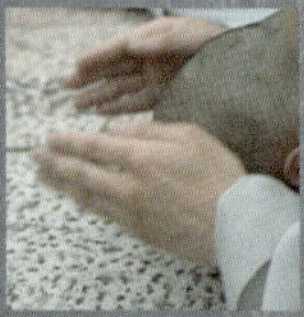

Musing From a Guide

Imagine there is a bottle filled to the brim with putrid slime. No one can drink it and the foul smell alone is enough to make one frown. If you are full of worries and annoyances due to something or somebody, your mind is like the sewage water in the bottle. It does not help you or help others. It would be best to throw it away as soon as possible.

However, it is not as easy to empty the grimes out of your mind as you think. You have to remove the cap from the bottle. Otherwise, no matter how you tip the bottle, nothing comes out. Open up your heart if you want to empty your mind of all the defilements. If you do not acknowledge, accept and express them because of pride or shame, your mind will get sicker and sicker like the stale dirty water in the bottle that becomes rotten.

The Buddha is the most compassionate being in the universe. He never reproaches or condemns you. He never turns his face away or scowls no matter how foul smelling you are. So, pluck up your courage and confess to the Buddha, "Oh, Buddha, I have so much filth in my mind."

And lower your body as if tipping the bottle. But if you tip it only a little bit, the water will just slosh around. The more you tilt it, the emptier the bottle gets. As if toppling the bottle over, just throw yourself to the humblest place in the world. The more you bow, the lower you get, the more slop you can unload from the bottle. Bow until your body is soaked wet with sweat. You will be surprised to find how purified you are before you know it.

The Buddha is the wisest being in the universe. Once your mind is empty of dirt, he will fill the void with the clean water of wisdom. It is so fresh and pure that it will not only quench your thirst, but your neighbors' deprivation as well.

The Essence of the Korean Buddhism Practices

6 Ways to the Heart

First Editon December 26, 2011

Produced by	Association of Korean Buddhist Orders #46-22, Soosong-Dong, Jongno-Ku, Seoul, Korea Tel: +82-2-732-4885 Fax: +82-2-737-7872
Published by	Bulkwang Publishing #46-21, Soosong-Dong, Jongno-Ku, Seoul, Korea Tel: +82-2-420-3300 Fax: +82-2-420-3400
Written by	Seong Jae Hyeon
Translated by	Hong Yon Ju
Proofreading	Ross Chambers
Photos	Ha Ji Kwon

ISBN 978-89-7479-206-0 03220
US $18 ₩20,000